How To Tell If Your Lawyer is C.R.A.P.

The essential guide for all involved in civil litigation

Blair Nelson is not a Lawyer but an ordinary hard working individual. Nelson has over 14 years experience in observing and working with lawyers. The aim of this book is to help members of the public when they employ the services of Lawyers in civil litigation matters.

How To Tell If Your Lawyer is C.R.A.P.

The essential guide for all involved in civil litigation

B.J. Nelson

Arena Books

First published in 2015 by Arena Books
Arena Books
6 Southgate Green
Bury St. Edmunds
IP33 2BL

www.arenabooks.co.uk
**Distributed in America by Ingram International, One Ingram Blvd., PO Box
3006, La Vergne, TN 37086-1985, USA.**

B.J Nelson
> *How To Tell If Your Lawyer is C.R.A.P. The essential guide for all
> involved in civil litigation*

British Library cataloguing in Publication Data. A catalogue record for this Book is
available from the British Library.

ISBN-13   978-1-909421-85-1

BIC classifications: - LA, LAB, LAM, LASD, LAT, LATC.

Printed and bound by Lightning Source UK

Cover design
by Jason Anscomb

Typeset in
Times New Roman

CONTENTS

IMPORTANT NOTE

The book has been written based on the author's experience of Solicitors, legal professionals and the Justice System in England. References to the obligations of Solicitors are made in relation to the practice guidance of The Law Society of England and Wales and the SRA Code of Conduct.

One of the main purposes of this book is to provide readers with a template for an Agreement of their own to protect their interests which sets out clearly what to expect from their Solicitor, irrespective of the rules of their own Regulator/Law Society. The Agreement may be used by you whether you are using a Solicitor in England, Wales, Scotland and Northern Ireland (or indeed in any country where the legal system is founded on English Law).

Introduction

Why is it so rare to find anybody with a kind word to say about Lawyers?

Whether it is an issue about being charged too much in fees, poor service or the competence of the Lawyer in question, the fundamental reason is normally the failure of the Lawyer to meet the Client's expectations.

A very experienced Lawyer told me the cause of the problem. He said most members of the public think they can trust Lawyers to know what they are doing when they employ them. However, he said that, in his experience, 90% of litigation Lawyers are incompetent - so the public simply don't know if their Lawyer is one of the competent 10%!

Now, I am sure that some members of the legal profession would debate the percentages he used, but that does not detract from the strength of the point he was trying to make!

Employing a Lawyer for legal action is taking a giant leap into the unknown for many people. Most members of the public do not really know what they are letting themselves in for when employing Lawyers in litigation matters. Believe me, there are many important things you need to know before you place your faith and trust in these individuals and the legal system in which they work.

Now, I am going to clear something up first. When I use the term 'Lawyer' in this book, I am referring to what is traditionally known in the UK as a '**Solicitor**' – a member of the legal profession who people go to for legal advice. Solicitors are supposed to be competent, not only to advise Clients but also to instruct Barristers. This book is primarily about Solicitors because they are the professionals who the public rely on to handle their cases and communicate with them.

Almost everyone refers to Solicitors as 'Lawyers' these days. It is not necessarily wrong to call a Solicitor a Lawyer because they are people who practice in the 'Law' (along with other categories of people working in the legal profession). However, be careful because not all Lawyers are Solicitors and I will explain the significance of this later in the book.

This book has been written to help you understand how Solicitors work and what they are required to do for you when they act on your behalf in a civil lawsuit. The book has also been written to help you understand the practicalities of litigation itself.

After reading this book, you should:

- Be aware of the *'professional'* duties placed on Solicitors when acting for you and giving you advice (believe me when I say that *some* Solicitors don't even know these themselves).

- Be able to protect your interests by issuing an Agreement to bind your Solicitor to act in the way you want.

- Be better placed to make an informed choice on taking any legal action *before* you are committed to it.

Who is this book aimed at?

This book is aimed at any INDIVIDUAL or COMPANY seeking to know more about how Solicitors are supposed to act when giving advice and handling litigation when they employ their services.

The information contained in this book may be helpful to:

- People considering taking legal action against another party.

- People already in the process of taking legal action but want to be informed about what to expect from their Solicitor and what their Solicitor is required to do for them.

- People being sued by another party.

Why did I write this book?

I felt compelled to write this book as a result of a quite unbelievable experience my father had with a firm of Solicitors. The conduct and service of the firm was so poor that it left my father in financial ruin and ill health at a time in his life when he should have retired - all thanks to the inadequate advice and incompetent actions of an individual at the firm.

I do not want the introduction of this book taken up by me going off on a bitter sounding rant, so I won't go on about that. However, as the whole unsatisfactory situation unfolded, it became apparent to me that if my father had been made aware of basic facts and given proper and balanced advice by the firm of Solicitors, he would never have proceeded with the legal action. Accordingly, he would never have found himself in the position which the firm of Solicitors led him into.

During the course of the experience it also occurred to me that many people must also be in the same situation, in that their Solicitor may not be advising them properly either. I'm not for one moment saying that all Solicitors are incompetent or bad. Not at all. There are some good Solicitors out there. What I am saying is:

How do you know if you are really getting good advice?

How can you tell?

Will the Solicitor have the guts to tell you the *true* overall costs?

Will they explain the *true* risks?

Will they properly establish if the action is going to be of benefit to you rather than themselves?

Will they tell you *everything* before committing you to a course of action that you may later regret?

Bear in mind that a fundamental conflict exists between the interests of a litigation Solicitor and their Client. Often, the best advice the Solicitor should give to the Client is: *"Don't litigate or, if you must, bring it to an end as quickly and cheaply as possible"*. However, the best advice the Solicitor can give themselves is often: *"Spin the Client's litigation out as long and expensively as you can"*.

Now that Solicitors are more focused on business generation rather than being professionals, the practice of fee generation and fee churning are much more common today than in the past. This book is therefore designed to help you make sure that your Solicitor focuses on being a professional rather than focusing on the fees they want to charge you.

Obviously, I cannot comment precisely about your case or say categorically whether you are getting good advice (because every case is different and there may be many subjective legal issues and merits involved). However, there are certain minimum requirements which Solicitors have to meet and these are common to all litigation cases. Using these to test the advice received, will help you in your assessment of your Solicitor's performance.

I therefore want to help you decide for yourself by simply outlining key facts and inside information which some Solicitors may not have the courage or foresight to tell their Clients.

I want to arm you with the knowledge which my father never had so that you can be empowered to get the best out of your Solicitor and decide for yourself if the service you are receiving is satisfactory.

In that way, you will, at the very least, be in a position to make your decision on how to (or whether to) proceed with your case.

I also hope that this book will help Solicitors to understand the needs and expectations of Clients. In this way, the whole litigation experience can be improved for both the Solicitor and the Client.

The format of this book

This book contains a series of chapters setting out the main points which I believe you should be aware of, based on my experience of litigation. I have not set out to write a long book with an over-use of technical jargon. This is a book which you can easily read at your leisure.

However, as litigation is no easy walk in the park itself, this book is not a quick read – but I cannot help that!

Some of what I have learned about litigation and Solicitors' obligations comes from my study of the SRA Code of Conduct and practice rules of The Law Society. The rules and codes, which Solicitors are professionally obliged to comply with, cover different areas of practice and the rules are amended from time to time. From my experience, the rules and principles which apply to one area of practice also apply to other areas of practice. For example, you will see that there are constant references to 'Cost/Risk/Benefit analysis' and 'Client Care' in several different chapters. All will be revealed in the book.

The book is made up of a series of chapters covering important topics and each chapter is rounded off with additional 'tips' for you to keep in mind. A template of the 'Terms of Engagement' you might consider using appear after that. At the rear of the book is a Glossary of Terms to help you understand the commonly used phrases and legal terminology.

So, please don't think you need to memorise all the advice and regulations as you read the book. Once you have finished, you will know which parts are helpful to your situation. However, above all else, the 'Terms of Engagement' in Chapter 11 are provided for you to use in order to protect your interests.

CHAPTER 1

The Lottery of Litigation

So, you're either involved in legal action already or are thinking about it. Don't be under any illusion that it's going to be a pleasurable ride or a cheap one.

If you're not careful you can end up getting 'stung' because you were given unrealistic expectations on the chances of success and inadequate advice on the potential costs and risks. Having also learned about the experiences of other people who have taken legal action, it gives me no pleasure to say I am not the only person to think that way.

The majority of decent and trusting lay-people who get involved in litigation do so in the belief that the legal system will see justice done for them.

I certainly did.

I thought that all Solicitors protected the financial interests of their own Clients. If a case went to Court, I believed that, as long as the facts were relayed to the Court properly and you were honest, then everything would work out in the end. Being open, truthful and precise with the facts would provide the platform for victory.

I thought all Judges would be consistent, competent and fair. I thought that the Courts would therefore be able to tell black from white and common sense would prevail. The bad guys would lose and the good guys would win.

I had faith in the legal system and trusted in the ability of the legal professionals who were supposed to know what they were doing and to act in my family's best interests.

Why shouldn't any trusting person have those beliefs in the legal system? Such expectations are perfectly reasonable in any normal civilised society.

I was completely wrong to hold such beliefs and faith in the legal system.

I can tell you that there are many people who share the same dissatisfaction with their Solicitor and their legal journey as my father (even some people who have won their cases). In fact, many of these people, given the chance of going back in time, would never have wasted their time and money taking the legal action. The only real beneficiaries were the Solicitors and the other legal advisers employed.

Now, don't get me wrong and think I am being negative. I am not. I am being deliberately realistic as it is very important for you to be able to take a step back from the emotional attachment you may have to your case and keep an objective view. It's all too easy to get talked into taking a positive view of your case. You may find that you are told that you have a good case by your legal team and you end up proceeding but don't properly stop to think that your opponent will have a legal team of their own telling them a different story.

Legal action is often simply the consequence of a human desire to be understood: each party has their own side of the story to tell and they want someone else to see it their way. In a nutshell, that's why people take legal action. In reality, the "someone else" (a Judge) may not see things their way – so it's always best to approach litigation with caution. Much of your costs will be incurred paying others for trying to think of arguments to convince the Judge that you are right and your opponent is wrong. Get the right Judge on the right day and you will win. Get the wrong Judge on the wrong day and you will be disappointed.

Of course, there are some good Solicitors out there who will do an acceptable job for you (especially if they win your case when you will think they are the best Solicitors in the world). However, even the best Solicitor in the land will be the first to admit that managing expectations of success and controlling the outcome of your case is impossible. Your fate lies ultimately in the hands of that Judge and he (or she) may (or may not) understand or sympathise with your case. Therefore, it is fair to say that, on average, achieving success is no more certain than going into a betting shop and placing a bet on a horse.

Stop and consider this for a moment.

How many times does a race horse lose a race when it was originally tipped as the favourite to win?

ANSWER: It happens all the time.

Nobody can predict the result. Litigation is no different.

The only certain outcome is that you will have to pay out large sums of money to your Solicitor, Barrister and/or QC when they cannot even guarantee you victory themselves in return.

Is that fair?

Is that acceptable?

This is the crucial question you will have to decide for yourself.

I fully appreciate that there will be situations where some of us have little or no choice to take legal action (because you feel you have been wronged and have a valid case or because you are being sued and you have to defend yourself).

If you have to take legal action, then it is essential that your Solicitor gives you realistic expectations so you can decide if it is worth proceeding or not. Take it from someone who's been there and done it. Don't fall into the same traps my father did. Make sure the Solicitor does a proper job for you and prepares your case meticulously.

So, how do you do that?

The obvious answer is that it's the Solicitor's job – not yours! Before I had experience of litigation, I would have said that answer was unhelpful. However, it boils down to knowing what questions to ask of your Solicitor and knowing how to construct an Agreement of your own to protect your interests which will run alongside the 'Terms of Business' they will ask you to sign.

Being able to tell if your Solicitor is doing a good job is simpler than you might think. You have to be aware of:

1. The obligations placed upon your Solicitor by their own professional body.

2. Key aspects of the system in which your Solicitor works and how to counter any potential negatives which may otherwise affect your position.

In England and Wales, all Solicitors are required to follow the Principles and Codes of the **SRA (Solicitors Regulation Authority)**. Sticking to the **SRA Principles** is compulsory for all Solicitors. Solicitors are also required to follow the **SRA Code of Conduct** as well as the Practice Guidance of The Law Society.

[Just to help you, The Law Society in England and Wales is the professional association which represents Solicitors. The Law Society used to be responsible for regulating Solicitors. However, the regulatory powers were handed over to the SRA to maintain independence.

In Scotland and Northern Ireland, The Law Society in those respective countries regulate Solicitors]

Your Solicitor is therefore professionally bound to follow these codes/rules throughout all stages of your legal action. Your Solicitor is the key person in the process and has to adhere to their professional obligations of 'CLIENT CARE'.

Quite simply, the test for their advice should be:

If their own mother were in the same situation as you, would the Solicitor give her the same advice they are giving you?

A Solicitor should care for you in the same way that he (or she) would care for a member of their own family. That means your Solicitor should properly and fully advise you on all areas of the case so there are no nasty surprises at the end (i.e. no surprises over the possible result, no surprises over the final costs or any other aspect of the matter).

Before I proceed, I want to ask you if you know some interesting facts about legal action and Solicitors.

- Did you know that even if you win your case you will never get all your own costs back? A Solicitor is required to tell you this.

- Did you know that a professional duty of your Solicitor is to explore whether you have legal expenses insurance already in place and if not, the Solicitor should explore the possibility (and arrange) something called *after-the-event* insurance which covers you against the costs if you lose the case?

- Did you know that there are organisations which may be able to loan you the money to fund your case if you have that insurance in place? In other words, in some cases it is possible to take legal action and it will cost you relatively little if you lose.

- Did you know that if you discover that you've been over-charged by a Solicitor you cannot challenge the bill in Court via a cost 'Assessment' process if 12 months have passed from the date you paid it? Even if you discover the over-charge or a mistake it is unlikely that you will be able to do anything about it once the 12 months have elapsed. This is a unique privilege enjoyed by Solicitors and the legal profession. What is even more surprising about this is that, in a civil situation on any other matter, you would get 6 years from the date of the act to challenge it. One rule for the legal profession and another for us!

[Generally, a bill cannot be challenged after it has been paid but sometimes a Solicitor's bill can be challenged after payment as a right later in exceptional circumstances – but proving those exceptional circumstances can be a time consuming challenge in itself]

I don't know about you, but I found these incredible – but they are only a small selection of all the points I want to tell you about in this book. I wish I had known these before but sadly I found these out only after my father had been so poorly advised by the original firm of Solicitors.

Like I say, I will tell you more about the SRA Principles, the SRA, The Law Society and the necessity for a Solicitor to follow the rules later in the book. However, let me just tell you now that if a Solicitor ever tells you that the SRA Principles/Codes and Law Society rules are not serious requirements, then have nothing more to do with that Solicitor!

Whilst writing this book, I came across a Solicitor who told me that the Principles and Codes were not of major importance or significance. I was amazed – not just at what he said – but at the fact he was also a senior partner at a firm of Solicitors. I also met another Solicitor who arrogantly described the Principles and Codes as meaningless and unimportant. I was astonished to hear this coming from someone who was supposed to be an intelligent man.

CHAPTER 2

What is a Solicitor (Lawyer)?

Many people who use the services of a Solicitor are not aware of what a Solicitor actually is. Many people are also unaware of what a Solicitor is legally and professionally required to do for them when acting on their behalf.

A Solicitor is a qualified professional person who offers legal services to Clients. Generally, a Solicitor does not speak for a Client in a Court but will instruct a Barrister or a Q.C. to do so - although some Solicitors may be able to act as an advocate (someone who makes a case on behalf of another) in certain circumstances.

In order to become a Solicitor, the individual has to complete a formal set of qualifications as well as serving a minimum training contract with a firm of Solicitors. Individuals can only call themselves Solicitors if they have been *admitted* to practice by '**The Master of the Rolls**' (a senior Judge who admits Solicitors to practice and holds important duties in relation to public record keeping). A Solicitor must also hold a valid 'Practice Certificate' from the SRA or relevant The Law Society (unless they are exempt).

Any individual working at a firm of Solicitors who is not admitted and does not hold a Practice Certificate, is *NOT* a Solicitor. I make this point because it is a common misconception that individuals giving advice at Solicitor firms are Solicitors. That is not so.

For example, individuals at firms in those circumstances may be *Trainee Solicitors*, *Legal Executives* (who are not Solicitors but have to be qualified and have at least 5 years experience working under the supervision of a Solicitor), *Paralegals* (who carry out legal work in a supporting role such as preparing documents, research and clerical tasks) or *Clerks* (who assist Solicitors in the execution of their professional duties).

Take note that any individual who is not a Solicitor is deemed to be inexperienced and their work has to be supervised by the partners of the firm.

What is their basic duty?

A Solicitor's job is to provide a Client with 'advice' so the Client can decide how to proceed. A Solicitor's job is not to merely take instructions from a Client. This may seem an obvious thing to say but some Solicitors seem to think their job is to take instructions from their Client without giving them proper advice in return - and then blame the Client for the actions taken after it all goes wrong!

A Solicitor has a contractual duty of care to a Client and should not cause the Client 'wrong' or 'injury' (a 'tort' in legal terms). Solicitors are also bound by the rules of The Law Society or SRA when acting for Clients.

The compulsory basic duties of a Solicitor in England and Wales are set out below, as per SRA requirements:

1. A Solicitor must uphold the rule of law and the proper administration of justice.

2. A Solicitor must act with integrity.

3. A Solicitor must not allow their independence to be compromised.

4. A Solicitor must act in the best interests of the Client.

5. A Solicitor must provide a good standard of service to Clients.

6. A Solicitor must not behave in a way that is likely to diminish the trust the public places in their profession.

7. A Solicitor must comply with their legal and regulatory obligations and deal with their Regulators and Ombudsmen in an open, timely and co-operative manner.

8. A Solicitor must run their business or carry out their role in the business effectively and in accordance with proper governance and sound financial and risk management principles.

9. A Solicitor must run their business in a way that encourages equality of opportunity and respect for diversity.

10. A Solicitor must protect client money and assets.

These Principles are applicable to *all aspects* of a Solicitor's practice. Within the Principles above, there are additional requirements that a Solicitor has to meet. For example, a Solicitor must always 'act in good faith' and this principle binds the whole Solicitor/Client relationship. If a Solicitor gives you an 'undertaking' (i.e. makes a promise to do something or deal with something) then the Solicitor has to honour that undertaking. Equally as important, a Solicitor must not take unfair advantage of anyone.

More details on the rules/code of conduct will be highlighted in later chapters which correspond to the topics identified as important to you. Some of the rules/codes are repeated in different chapters due to the cross-over of duties a Solicitor has to fulfil in the different tasks they carry out.

If you wish to look up the Principles and Codes contained in the 'SRA Code of Conduct', these can be found at *www.sra.org.uk*. As mentioned earlier, this is the website of the **Solicitors Regulation Authority (SRA)** which is the independent regulatory arm of The Law Society in England and Wales.

If The Law Society was a cake, the SRA would be the top layer of the organisation where the issues of ultimate importance are dealt with. The purpose of the SRA is to protect the public by ensuring that Solicitors meet high standards. If you need guidance you should contact The Law Society (for contact details please see Chapter 10). For those of you who do not reside in England or Wales please contact the relevant Law Society to your country or region.

The use of the term 'Lawyer'

The word 'Lawyer' is a loosely used term to describe someone working in the legal profession. It seems to have originated from the United States of America. As I mentioned earlier, in the minds of most lay-people, the words 'Lawyer' and 'Solicitor' mean the same thing (because we assume that the person has achieved qualifications to become a 'Lawyer' or a 'Solicitor'). However, do *not* automatically assume that people calling themselves 'Lawyers' are actually 'Solicitors'. Remember, they have to be *admitted* and hold a Practice Certificate from SRA or their Law Society after they have achieved the requisite qualifications and have the appropriate experience.

Conflicts of Interest

A Solicitor must not act if there is a conflict of interests. A conflict of interest can be said to exist if:

- The Solicitor (or the firm) owes separate duties to act in the best interests of 2 or more Clients in relation to the same case.

- There is a significant risk that those duties may conflict.

- The Solicitor's duty to act in the best interests of any Client in respect of the matter conflicts, or there is a significant risk fact it may conflict with the Solicitor's own interests in relation to that matter.

Under the rules, a Solicitor has a duty to remove themselves from your case if a conflict of interest exists. There may be certain situations where a firm of Solicitors may act for 2 or more Clients but the Solicitor must draw your attention to all the relevant issues *before* agreeing to act (or where they are already acting, they must bring it to your attention immediately). A Solicitor must be able to demonstrate that you have understood all the relevant issues in respect of a conflict of interest.

Duty of Confidentiality

A Solicitor must keep your affairs confidential at all times (even after your case has ended). The only exception to this rule is where disclosure is required or permitted by law or if you give your consent to release the information.

Duty of Disclosure

A Solicitor must disclose to you all information which they are aware of which is material to your case, regardless of the source of information, subject to:

- The duty of confidentiality (above) which always overrides the duty of disclosure *(however, there are situations where Solicitors need to be careful – as in a case where a firm of Solicitors acted for both the 'seller' and 'purchaser' and did not tell one Client relevant information they learned from the other Client. The Solicitor felt obliged not to disclose it, according to their duty of confidentiality – but the House of Lords confirmed that their duty of disclosure was not overridden when they knew that a conflict of interest existed).*

- The following where the duty does not apply:
- *where such disclosure is forbidden by law*
- *where it has been expressly agreed that no duty to disclose exists (or a different standard of disclosure applies)*
- *where the Solicitor reasonably believes that a serious physical or mental injury will be caused to any person if the information is disclosed to you*

Management of the firm's business

Rules exist which require firms of Solicitors to properly supervise and manage their own staff. These rules relate specifically to the firm's own internal procedures to ensure that their staff act competently and properly when delivering their service to Clients. Supervision and management refers to the professional overseeing of staff and Client matters. Broadly, the rules aim to:

- Identify the responsibility for the overall supervision and management structures in place at the firm.

- Set the minimum requirements to be met in order to be 'qualified to supervise'.

- Set the minimum standards which apply to the supervision of your case itself.

- Set the minimum requirements in relation to the firm's business arrangements which are considered to be essential to good practice and integral to compliance with supervision and other duties to you.

Monitor the time you spend talking to your Solicitor

In my view, Solicitors lead a very privileged and charmed existence where they believe they are justified in charging for their time speaking to you. However, most people in their daily jobs do not get paid for just talking to someone or writing them a report. People generally only get paid if a sale is made or a project comes to fruition which can involve a great deal of work beforehand. All that work can be for nothing if the business is not placed or the contract is not won. Generally, in the world of the average Solicitor, as soon as they spend time doing something for you, their clock starts ticking and fees are run up, even if it's for a simple administrative matter.

Many Solicitors have a built-in inflation factor to their charges. They charge in 'units' of time (ranging between 6 to 12 minutes per unit). It is not unusual for a firm of Solicitors to charge a unit of time for putting a letter in the post-room, another unit for reading and sending a copy by email, another unit for telephoning to check that the letter has been received and doing much the same on other cases for other Clients.

So, a Solicitor may charge multiple units of time for work which has actually been completed in a single unit. So watch out!

Speaking from personal experience, I can say categorically that the majority of Solicitors I have ever come into professional contact with, possessed an over-inflated idea of the value of their worth to my family as a Client and held an exaggerated belief in their own abilities. They went to great lengths talking to us, telling us what they were going to do for us, making great play of what they were going to achieve. However, in reality, they ended up not doing what they said they would do and never succeeded in what they set out to achieve. Now, I'm not saying that all Solicitors are like this – but please be warned!

I mean, how do you know whether the advice you have received is of sufficient quality to be chargeable?

It's an imperfect and, in some cases, an unfair way of operating.

If they are going to charge you £250 plus VAT per hour (or £300 or £400 or £1,000 or whatever it is they choose), how on earth are they able to prove that every pound has been properly and justifiably earned? How many hours are they going to have to spend on the case?

When they've charged for 'X' hours of work, how do you know what they were doing for each minute of those hours?

Making themselves a coffee?

Getting a snack?

Chatting to a colleague?

Unnecessarily duplicating time and fees by re-reading the same parts of the file over again?

Quite honestly, from my experience of Solicitors (and the experience of other people I have spoken to who have employed them), if they had only been paid half of their desired hourly rate it would have still have been more that they actually deserved.

Without exception, the litigation Solicitors who have acted for my family in 6 years may as well have charged for 'farting'. The hot air which came out of that end of their anatomy was of higher quality than the garbage which came out of their mouths. The saying 'talking out their arse' could not be more appropriate! On occasions you may find yourself having to take time to speak to your Solicitor, explaining something to them or educating them on a particular aspect of your case or situation where they have no knowledge themselves.

Is it right they should charge you for educating them?

I personally do not think it is right – but it's a debate which could go on for ages. However, imperfect though the system may be, it is important that you keep your telephone call lengths down to the minimum – and keep a record of how long you spend talking to them.

I would also like to say that, from the years I have worked with Solicitors in England, I sincerely believe that litigation Solicitors acting for Claimants should only be paid on a 'results' basis. If they lose the case they should get nothing (and the same goes for Barristers and Q.C.'s). Or, at the very least, a mechanism should exist whereby they only get paid based on what they achieve (i.e. in comparison to what they set out to achieve at the outset). This would reduce the number of poorly prepared cases brought because Solicitors, Barristers and Q.C.'s would have to be sure of the advice they give before committing a Client to an action or they should be prepared to share some of the risk in the action itself.

I accept that it is slightly different if you are a Defendant because you will need to take the necessary steps to protect yourself and the Solicitor will do what they can to help. There is something fundamentally wrong with a system or profession where a person (or organisation) is financially rewarded regardless of whether they succeed or fail for a Client. There is also something inherently wrong about a profession where it can cost more in legal fees than the value of a claim which a person may wish to pursue.

For example, if you are owed £30,000 by another party, you should not have to incur £60,000 in legal costs to pursue that party – and then not be allowed to recover all of your costs at the end!

The legal profession does not always seem to be able to offer a service which directly fits the needs and circumstances of each client.

Solicitors should also not be permitted to charge fees in excess of the value of a claim they are pursuing – and certainly not charge fees which are more than is reclaimable in damages from the other party.

Sadly, they often do! A good example of the perverse nature of the profession is brilliantly demonstrated by the experience of a lady involved in a divorce case. She used a Solicitor for a divorce case where the only asset she possessed was her half share in the matrimonial home. When the divorce was concluded, her Solicitor's bill was higher than the value of her share in the home. She was left with nothing at the end of the process and might as well not have bothered using a Solicitor!

I believe the current system of fee charging needs reforming urgently - but that's another whole new debate. However, I would like to fuel that debate by saying that the practice of Solicitors charging hourly rates should be scrapped. Such a practice rewards inefficiency, poor service and incompetence.

A system of fixed charges should be introduced to replace it. Whether you are a Claimant or a Defendant, a Solicitor should only charge a fixed fee. One of the major flaws with hourly charging is that it treats 'time' as the item being sold to a Client. That cannot be right as it should be the skill, experience and efficient service which are sold to a Client. A fixed fee system would encourage efficiency amongst Solicitors and rid the industry of the uncontrolled spiralling costs syndrome and provide further cost control for Legal Aid work. The measure would also bring significant advantages to the after-the-event insurance market (see Chapter 6) because it would make costs more controllable and remove the element of risk where costs would not be allowed to spiral into the unknown.

A fixed fee system would also rid the legal profession of the dreadful practice whereby wealthy parties deliberately run up costs to drain their opposition of funds so they cannot continue with cases against them – resulting in the opposing parties being denied their right to justice.

The expense of litigation has always been one of the major problems with the civil justice system. The high costs are fuelled by the highly fierce 'battle like' environment in which litigation is normally conducted.

Reform of Civil Litigation Costs

A major step in the reform of legal costs was brought into effect in April 2013 as a result of a review and report conducted by a Lord Justice Jackson. Lord Justice Jackson specifically stated in his report:

> "In some areas of civil litigation costs are disproportionate and impede access to justice. I therefore propose a coherent package of interlocking reforms, designed to control costs and promote access to justice."

As a result, a process called **'Costs Budgeting'** has been introduced into the legal profession. This is supposed to make the cost of litigation and access to justice more manageable because both parties have to provide a 'Costs Budget' to the Court soon after the case is lodged in the Court. This regime of 'Costs Budgeting' is a welcome development and goes a long way to reforming the old problem of excessive fee charging by Lawyers. However, it is not without flaws and I will discuss this later on.

Observations & Tips

- Make sure the person you are dealing with is actually a Solicitor (not a Clerk, Paralegal or Legal Executive). Specifically *ask* for a Solicitor on making your first approach to a firm.

- Ask how long the Solicitor has been qualified.

- Ask what type of litigation they have experience in.

- Ask for details of specific cases and what costs were involved. Does their experience sound as if it would suit your case?

- Ask to see copies of the Judgments for cases in which they claim to have been involved. What was the outcome? Did the Judge criticise or compliment how the case was presented? The *www.bailii.org.uk* website can also prove helpful sometimes when you want to obtain a copy of a Judgment for yourself.

- Ask how many of their last 10 completed cases they have won in comparison to how many they have lost (i.e. ask for their **win/loss ratio**). Better to discover this at the outset rather than after you have progressed further with your case.

- There is a natural tendency to believe your Solicitor when they say *'we're going to achieve X, Y and Z'*. Well, don't. Nothing is guaranteed, despite any positive talk. Always keep a sense of realism.

- Be wary if a Solicitor ever praises himself or herself for the work they have done. Also, be wary of Solicitors if they tell you how good they are. They are only as good as the result they achieve for you – so never assume anything until the case is over. You can then judge for yourself how good they have been for you.

- Ask your Solicitor to send you copies of all notes of telephone calls, meetings with people, emails sent and received in relation to your case. Ask for this information to be sent at the outset and on an ongoing basis. This is so that you will know exactly what is going on. Make sure that they send you copies of everything, including communications from your opponent's Solicitors.

- *Never* be friends with your Solicitor. Always keep your relationship businesslike.

- *Never* compliment or praise your Solicitor for the job they do. They are paid by you to do a good job. Only compliment or praise your Solicitor *after* your case is over and you have won. If you compliment them (however innocently) during the case, they may try to use it in defence against any negligence action you later take against them.

- Litigation Solicitors should be regarded as no different from salesmen. Some are about selling you the 'idea' that your problem may be resolved by the legal solutions they suggest - as if they have a special legal 'toolbox' which they can go to and pull out an instrument to fix the problem. Like any goods or services you consider buying from a sales person, think seriously whether you actually need (or want) what they are attempting to sell you. Do not be influenced just because you might hear what they want you to hear. In many cases, the solutions/legal advice which they give are sometimes nothing more than thoughts and ideas based on hope and their personal interpretation of the law, with no guarantee of success.

CHAPTER 3

'Client Care'

A Solicitor is professionally bound by their duty of 'Client Care' - to look after you from start to finish. Fundamental to 'Client Care' is that your Solicitor is required to act in your best interests at all times and treat you with fairness and respect.

The old fashioned principle of 'the Client is King' is what should govern all Solicitors. Sadly, that principle seems to be a rarity these days. Money and hitting fee targets is what now appears to drive many Solicitor firms.

'Client Care' covers a number of areas such as:

- Your Solicitor knowing what your objectives are.

- What you are told by your Solicitor at the outset and throughout the matter.

- Information on costs and risks.

- On-going advice in general.

The presumption a Solicitor must adopt from the outset is that you know nothing about litigation or how Solicitors are supposed to advise you. In other words, you are coming to your Solicitor 'blind' to the risks, costs and ways of the system in which litigation works. Therefore, it is your Solicitor's job to 'open your eyes' and inform you of what to expect and what is required. Your Solicitor must only lead you into legal action with your 'eyes wide open'.

Equally fundamental to 'Client Care' is that a Solicitor must understand what you are seeking to achieve by taking any potential legal action.

Under the 'Client Care' rule a Solicitor must:

- Identify clearly your objectives in relation to the work to be done.

- Give a clear explanation of the issues involved (especially costs, risks and benefits) and the options available to you.

- Agree with you what steps are to be taken (if any).

- Keep you informed of the progress on your case.

- Agree an appropriate level of service at the outset (and throughout, as required).

- Explain their responsibilities.

- Explain your responsibilities.

- Ensure that you are given the name and status of the person dealing with your case (and the name of the person responsible for its overall supervision). This must be provided in writing.

- Explain any limitations or conditions resulting from their relationship with a third party which might affect the steps they can take on your behalf.

Solicitors adopt different approaches to the provision of 'Client Care'. A decent Solicitor should send you a 'CLIENT CARE LETTER' explaining the key areas (not only in terms of what you can expect from them in the way of service but also spell out the potential costs and risks of any potential legal action).

Some Solicitors put 'Terms of Business' or 'Terms and Conditions' in their 'Client Care' letters. Others write shorter letters and attach separate 'Terms and Conditions'. Either way, these documents must contain the requisite information to comply with the rules.

In reality, a good 'Client Care' letter issued by a Solicitor (whether it is supplied on its own or with separate 'Terms and Conditions'), should:

- Clearly identify you (as the Client) and your objectives in the legal matter.

- State what your Solicitor is instructed to do (giving time-scales, if possible).

- Give an *overall* estimate of costs for the matter (broken down by fees, VAT and payments to third parties).

- Give a clear explanation of the issues in question and the extent of the retainer (i.e. your agreement to pay fees in return for the Solicitor acting for you).

- Give the name and status of the person dealing with your case in the firm (and the name of the principal responsible for its overall supervision).

- Give the name and status of the person who you should approach if there is a problem or you have a complaint (and that you have the option to refer matters to the Legal Ombudsman, how to do it and timescales etc).

- Advise you of the COST/RISK/BENEFIT analysis for pursuing your case (i.e. what is the point of spending £1 if you are only going to get 10p back or nothing at all?). In other words, a Solicitor *must* discuss with you whether the potential outcome of the case will justify the expense or risk involved including, if relevant, the risk of having to pay your opponent's costs.

- Explain that you have a right to set an upper limit on fees .

- Explain that the Solicitor will explore the possibility of arranging insurance for you to cover your costs in the event that you lose the case.

- Advise the terms of the charges they make.

- Advise you if the charging rates are to be increased.

- Advise of the likely payments you may need to make to third parties.

- Give confirmation that the Solicitor will discuss with you your ability to pay and how you will do so (i.e. whether you may be eligible for public funding via Legal Aid or whether it is possible to obtain funding using an insurance policy referred to above).

- Advise you that there may be circumstances where the Solicitor will be entitled to hold your files in the event of unpaid costs (referred to as a 'Lien').

- That, even if you win your case, the other party may not be ordered to pay costs (or may even not be in a position to pay them at all).

- That any information about costs (both in the present and future) will be confirmed in writing.

In *all* cases, a Solicitor must discuss how the costs are to be met and whether you are eligible for Legal Aid. If your Solicitor does not do Legal Aid work they must still explain the advantages of Legal Aid (if you are eligible) and give you the chance to approach a Solicitor who does Legal Aid work.

Different Solicitors will phrase the above bullet-point information in different ways. However, it is important to carefully study the 'Client Care' letter and any 'Terms and Conditions' when you receive them. The information contained in the bullet points in this chapter are just minimum standards a Solicitor should meet. You will see from the following chapters that there is a whole lot more which will enable you to make sure you are properly cared for.

It is important to remember that 'Client Care' does *not* stop after a letter and 'Terms and Conditions' are issued by a Solicitor. 'Client Care' has to be maintained throughout your case.

Once you have read this book you will not just have to rely on what your Solicitor tells you (or what they do not) in respect of your 'Client Care'.

In order to protect your interests further from any potential inadequate advice or service received from your Solicitor, this book will provide you with 'Terms of Engagement' of your own to run alongside those you will be asked to sign by your Solicitor. This will maximise the chances of you receiving an acceptable level of 'Client Care' over and above the basic requirements of the rules.

For your information, the duty of a Solicitor to advise a Client is summed up in the case of *County Personnel Ltd v Allen R Pulver & Co (1987) I WLR 916.* A Solicitor's duty is to provide appropriate advice with appropriate force and in the appropriate language. Lord Justice Bingham said in that case:

> "It seems obvious that legal advice, like any other communication, should be in terms appropriate to the comprehension and experience of the particular recipient. It is also, I think, clear that in a situation such as this the professional man does not necessarily discharge his duty by spelling out what is obvious. The client is entitled to expect the exercise of a reasonable professional judgment. That is why the client seeks advice from the professional man in the first place. If in the exercise of a reasonable professional judgment a solicitor is or should be alerted to risks which might elude even an intelligent layman, then plainly it is his duty to advise the client of these risks or explore the matter further."

In simple terms, this means that a Solicitor has to consider a Client's case in detail and advise them of all the risks and relevant issues because the Solicitor is the professional. The Solicitor should never assume that a Client will know the obvious. The Solicitor has to do the work and spell everything out. Otherwise, what's the point of the Client going to see a Solicitor for advice in the first place?

The above is further supported by a case called ***Crossnan v Ward Bracewell & Co (1989) 4 PN 103*** where it was found that, even if advice is given to a Client but the advice is incomplete, then the Solicitor will have been negligent in his professional duty to the Client.

Observations & Tips

- Always carefully read the 'Client Care' letter you are sent along with any 'Terms and Conditions' or 'Terms of Business'.

- Do not accept the terms in the letter or in the conditions as 'one-way traffic' as far as your own obligations are concerned.

- Issue your Solicitor with 'Terms of Engagement' of your own to run along side theirs (see Chapter 11).

- On day one, purchase a diary for the specific purpose of keeping notes on your case. A **day-on-a-page** diary is preferable. Make notes of every conversation you have with your Solicitor throughout your case. Also, make a note of the time you spend on the telephone with them or at meetings. It will prove invaluable to you as the case progresses (as you can not only remind your Solicitor of what they have previously advised you but you will see if they start to contradict themselves in later advice they may provide).

- I repeat, you must request that your Solicitor sends you copies of all their telephone notes, notes of meetings with third parties and any file note they make along the way. You can then keep the same file as they have, so you can be better informed on how your case is progressing.

- Ask what experience your Solicitor has in dealing with cases like yours. In my experience, litigation Solicitors are not always experts in the field you need them to be – there is an element of you having to educate them on details of your profession or situation – remember, you will end up having to pay them for the time you spend educating them!

- The sign of a good Solicitor is their ability to be able to give advice which a Client may not want to hear. A bad Solicitor is one who will tell a Client what they want to hear and then back-track when the case goes to Court!

- Ask your Solicitor if they would be prepared to fix their fees for the job. Depending on the nature of your case, they may be able to agree to this. However, Solicitors are professionally obligated to inform you of the option to have an upper limit set on your fees.

- Be wary of situations where Solicitors may charge you for sorting out a problem/complication which they have caused themselves. For example, they may not have dealt with a matter when they should have done or not liaised with Counsel on their fees etc. If they have to spend time rectifying the problem or resolving issues which would not otherwise have arisen if they had done their job properly, then there is no reason for you to be charged.

- Always make a note of any instructions you give your Solicitor over the telephone as well as note comments that *you* make. Time and date everything and retain it in your file/diary.

- If possible, record all telephone calls you have with your Solicitor. You will need to tell them that you are doing this. However, it will not only prove to be an invaluable source of reference in the future, but it may make them focus their own mind on giving you proper legal advice. If you do not have a telephone call recorder, try a company called **Re-Tell**. This company can supply a simple external device for your home phone or a more sophisticated device for the office (I am sure there are other suppliers of such devices, so shop around). **Re-Tell** can be contacted in the UK on **01932 730890** [or + 44 (0) 1932 730890 if you are calling from outside the UK]. Their website address is *www.retellrecorders.co.uk*.

- Be wary of confident Solicitors with a gung-ho style who believe that adopting an aggressive stance against your opponent will benefit your case or get you anywhere. These types of Solicitors can land you in serious financial trouble and give you a false impression that success is a foregone conclusion. Remember, a good Solicitor is one who will caution you of the risks and costs and will tell you that litigation and seeking resolution in Court should only be done as a last resort.

CHAPTER 4

Your Case

and

Your Relationship with Your Solicitor

U nless you've had experience of litigation before, you won't know how the relationship with your Solicitor will develop or how your case might pan out. It's fair to say that you probably won't know what you are in for.

To be frank, as no case is ever the same, it's impossible to say how your matter will develop and how your relationship with your Solicitor will go. However, if I tell you about my own experience and the experience of other people I have spoken to, I think it will give you a fair idea about what you should expect and prepare yourself for.

The required ingredients for a case to exist

Above all else, your case must have the essential components to make it stand up in Court. Without the requisite ingredients you should give up. If you are the party taking the action (the Claimant) the logical way to test whether your case has the requisite ingredients is to ask the following questions:

1. Did you have a contract with, or was a duty owed to you by, the person/body you are suing?

2. Has there been a breach of that duty or contract?

3. Has the breach caused the loss you are complaining of?

4. Is it too late to claim?

If the answer to the first three questions is 'Yes', then you have a potential case. If the answer to any of the first three questions is 'No' then you don't.

If you are the person defending yourself against an action (the Defendant), then the prospect of a solid defence is essentially the reverse side of the same coin. In other words, you should ask yourself the following questions:

1. Did you have a contract with, or did you owe a duty to, the other party?

2. Did you breach it?

3. Did the breach cause the loss which the other party is complaining of?

4. Is their claim time-barred (i.e. legally out of time for an action to be brought?).

If the answer to the first three questions is 'No' then you have a prospect of successfully defending yourself. If the answer to the first three questions is 'Yes', then you probably don't have much of a legal leg to stand on. If it is time-barred you have a defence.

The relationship with your Solicitor

Solicitors are a varied bunch. Some work for large city firms where the company culture is quite different from a Solicitor working in provincial areas or local villages with a different outlook on the legal system and cases they take on. Of course, you can probably say that about any profession but it should be remembered that any Solicitor, whether they are working for the biggest law firm in the country or the smallest one-man band, must adopt the same minimum standards in their approach when taking on a case and acting for you. As I said already, 'Client Care' should always be the order of the day.

So, you've walked through the door of your Solicitor's office and met them for the first time. You are telling yourself that he or she must be a good person and hope they are the right one to fight your corner and win your case.

In the early stages of the relationship with your Solicitor, you may well find that you even feel 'relieved' and 'content' because someone else appears to believe in your case enough to fight it or defend it. You may even find yourself thinking positively because your Solicitor agrees with your views on the case. You may hear a lot of 'bullish' and 'upbeat' talk and how they are going to give your opponent a really hard time.

Your optimism may even grow when you receive a positive initial opinion from a Barrister or Q.C. on your prospects. At this stage, if you have received positive advice, you will probably be happy to invest further money in the case because you have heard other people who are seeing it your way. They are telling you what you want to hear. At this point, you may be feeling good enough to have faith and even more trust in your Solicitor.

Well, hold on!

My advice to anyone would be: remain cautious and don't get too carried away. Unless you have a completely 'open and shut' case (which I'm told is quite rare because no case, regardless of how good it looks on paper, is ever without its potential difficulties), it is important to keep your feet anchored to the ground.

I would say that for most people it is highly likely that your relationship with your Solicitor will be filled with moments where you agree and disagree with him/her. The honeymoon period obviously starts at the beginning but it may turn into a sort of professional 'love hate' relationship. Not hate in the falling out sense (hopefully!) – but more like frustration when things don't go how your Solicitor originally said they might (or they don't do what they said they would do).

You should prepare yourself for the fact that your satisfaction with your Solicitor will be like a swinging pendulum, going from good to moderate to bad at any one point in time.

A typical example of how a relationship may develop between a Client and a Solicitor is as follows:

You go and see the Solicitor and he or she takes on your case because they think it's a good one. You feel great because you have gone to see them in the belief that you will see justice done and they are the experts – so you follow their advice because they are the professionals who know what to do. You put yourself entirely in their hands. You feel confident and positive because they give you words of comfort. Your Solicitor will be working to secure the evidence you need to prove that you're in the right. Along the way, they will come up with observations that they feel may help or harm your case (this is all part of the process).

Your Solicitor will probably come up with examples of other cases in law where Judgments have been given which appear to support your own case. This will make you feel even more secure because the law appears to be on your side and the case law can be used at trial to convince the Judge that you are right.

Your opponent's Solicitors will come up with arguments to counter your case (and these may drive you crazy because you know the points they make or things they say are invalid or not true). While all this is going on, you will be running up fees, which you may convince yourself are justified to fight your cause.

You may be told that getting the case resolved before it gets to trial is a possibility (through 'mediation' which the Courts these days now actively encourage). That may happen or it may not, but nobody can tell.

As the case progresses, you get to the stage where your Solicitor is able to issue your 'Claim' in Court (the detail of which will be typed up in what is called a 'Particulars of Claim' - POC) or issue your 'Defence' and possible 'Counter-Claim' if you are being sued. The claim will be based on what they have been able to establish at that point (but this information may not be complete because, as the case progresses, more information can come to light which causes your POC or Defence to have to be amended – which all costs money).

More blows are exchanged between parties along the way and you spend even more money on fees. You may find that your opponent applies to 'Strike-Out' your claim (i.e. get the Court to dismiss it before it gets to trial – a process known as 'Summary Judgment'). You are possibly still feeling positive and then you get to the point where 'Disclosure' of documents/evidence occurs. Both parties eventually exchange 'witness statements' where you get the opportunity to put the facts of your case down on paper and sign a statement of truth.

Your Solicitor may observe some new weaknesses in your case as a result of the disclosure process (or you discover that what you've previously been told, as far as all the positive talk is concerned, is now not as positive), but you've spent all this money so you feel there's a case to continue with. This may be aided by the encouraging advice you receive on the positive parts of your case - and so it may go on until you reach the point where you know the date for the trial. Then your Solicitor will find out who the Judge is going to be and they will start to research the Judge's background, like:

What cases has the Judge done before?

If the Judge was a Q.C. before, what area of practice did they specialise in?

All this is to find out whether you've got a Judge who may help you!

At this point, you may even find that your Solicitor starts to back-track on the things they've said in the past when they had previously built your hopes up. You may even find that your Solicitor is less confident on specific aspects of your case where they were previously positive – and it will drive you nuts! Your Solicitor's words of comfort given to you at the beginning of the case may suddenly (for no good reason) turn into words of discomfort by the time the trial begins. I would explain this feeling as one you may have experienced when you have studied for years, preparing for an exam. When the exam day comes, your teacher may worry because they realise that, for all the work you have put in, they have no control on the questions which will come up – and there's a chance you may fail. I suppose it is a natural human tendency to think like that when the big day arrives – but not when you've invested so much money in your case and when the people you've employed are supposed to know what they are doing.

You can find that your Solicitor at this stage starts to 'hedge their bets' as the trial day approaches in the realisation of the day of reckoning advances. It can be like a paranoia in their minds which comes from nowhere (and with no justification).

They can start to lower their sights from the original objectives which were supposed to be achieved (i.e. a lower damages figure or a partial success instead of a full one). Or they may have back-tracked on the number of witnesses originally identified for your case because they were not able to obtain witness statements within the deadline for statement exchange (or your Solicitor may have become distracted by the demands of other cases and no time has been left to fine tune statements or obtain further helpful evidence for yours – so it just becomes one big watered-down series of compromises). Once the documents have been exchanged between parties and the witness statements submitted – that's it. Those documents are the documents you are stuck with and will form the basis of your case.

I would describe that experience as one an athlete might feel when his coach tells him he should win a 'gold' medal and then on the day of the race says he may only win 'bronze'. The thing is that you are never really told at the beginning of the case that you only get one real chance to nail it at the trial. I sincerely believe Clients should be told this right at the beginning of the retainer with a Solicitor, rather than find out later when they have spent considerable sums of money and cannot pull out.

You may say to yourself, what am I doing being charged all this money on the case?

You also may say to yourself, where is the Solicitor's unnecessary paranoia coming from?

You suddenly discover that, for all the positive talk, all the positive legal advice you have received counts for very little.

Why?

Because all the legal advice provided by your Solicitor (based on their interpretation of the law with a Barrister or Q.C.) over the previous weeks, months or years is about to be finally tested.

And who is going to decide the result of the test? Who is going to accept or reject the legal arguments put forward by your Counsel in Court?

It's all down to that Judge and whether he or she is going to agree with your legal team - a human being in a fancy dress costume (usually) with robes and a wig is what stands between victory or defeat for you. And that's what it all boils down to. A human being requiring the use of a lavatory on a regular basis, just like any other member of the human race. A human being who is fundamentally no different from other human beings on the planet and one who does not always have the answers to every question put before them.

Once at trial when the case gets underway, will your Barrister or Q.C. perform well or to your expectations?

Will they ask all the questions you want them to?

Will a witness, supposedly put on a stand to help you, actually harm your case by saying something wrong?

Are you prepared for cross-examination in the witness box yourself (and how the opposing Barrister will twist the facts of a situation and twist what you say in order to portray a different picture)?

Will you be prepared for the negative feelings you will get when the Judge doesn't accept the case law being put forward by your Counsel?

Will you be prepared if it all goes wrong?

If the legal arguments used by your Counsel are not accepted by the Judge, all you will have achieved is shelling out money to your Solicitor and Counsel to come up with legal arguments which hold no legal credibility (i.e. If the legal arguments are not accepted by the Court then all those expensive legal arguments put forward by your Counsel just become a set of their own personal legal ideas, thought up to justify your case). If your case fails, the legal advice you have been provided amounts to nothing more than that: a set of legal ideas.

Will you then be prepared for your Solicitor putting a spin on the reasons why the case was lost?

In my experience, the Solicitors I have been involved with have possessed an amazing gift for trying to make you feel responsible for the failings of the advice they gave you! They said things like *'oh, we didn't see that one coming'* or *'we made the wrong choice'* or the like. You may hear the phrase *'let's not beat ourselves up about* it'. You may also hear your Solicitor say *'oh, bad luck but we did our best, didn't we?'*. Be prepared for this because they can start to use the word 'we' after a loss occurs when prior to the loss it was always *'I advise you .....'* You can be made to feel as if you are being taken on a collective guilt trip so they feel less awkward when it comes to demanding their fee payments – either that or you will find that they try to blame the Judge!

I recall a very unsatisfactory experience in my father's case with his Solicitor. Before the trial the Solicitor said that specific things were going to be done and achieved. Yet, after the trial he suddenly developed a very poor memory. Some of the answers he came up with when we queried matters were astonishing. So absurd in fact, that he would probably have tried to tell an Arab that sand did not exist in the desert – just to suit his own conscience!

An experience you may also have is when you get to the end of the case and you see what you have been charged overall. The bill will be one thing but when you analyse exactly what work was done, it may be hard to see how the Solicitor can justify the amount you have been billed for. Your Solicitor might try to claim that the reason for the bill being so high is because the case took so long to conclude (i.e. it may have been strung out for two years or more). In fact, when the work done is actually stripped out of the bill, it could probably have been done in no more than a week. During the years the case lasted, much of the time taken for the case to progress may simply have been due to the slow moving nature of the legal system itself. Your Solicitor may not have been working on your case every day because there was no need to do so. In reality, your Solicitor may have actually spent much of their time revisiting the same ground or issues which had already been identified and dealt with in the early stage of the case – simply because he or she had forgotten what originally occurred during those periods of inactivity when they had been working on other people's cases!

On the other hand, if you win the case, you will be on cloud nine and think your Solicitor is the best thing since sliced bread. **I really do hope the latter is your experience – but just be aware.**

Obviously, what I've said above will not happen in that way on every case – but you can bet it will for some – or something very similar.

In essence, legal action is rather like taking part in a boxing match. Two sides set out to beat each other and exchange blows along the way in a series of rounds. Some are just 'jabs' which don't harm and some are more serious 'body blows'. One side will try to trip up the other by employing their tactics while on their way to the final round. Which side is going to deal the final blow which knocks out their opponent?

A good Solicitor will prepare you for fighting that boxing match. So, look upon taking legal action (or defending yourself against legal action) as a boxing match with your Solicitor as the trainer in your corner. The outcome of the battle will never be certain until it's all over.

When it comes to the trial itself, expect the fight to be dirty with your opponent's Counsel trying to discredit you with points that are not true or facts taken out of context. Litigation is a nasty business and you should be under no illusions as to how difficult, stressful and expensive it can be.

What if you discover that your Solicitor is not actually a Solicitor?

If you discover that the individual handling your case at the firm is not a Solicitor then you should complain immediately. For example, you may discover that the individual is only a Clerk. If you have specifically asked for a Solicitor to handle your case and you were referred to someone who was not a Solicitor without your knowledge, then you have every right to demand your money back. This is supported by a case *Pilbrow v Pearless De Rougemont (1999) 3 All E R 355* where Lord Justice Schiemann at paragraph 360 point g said:

> "... In my judgment, a firm of solicitors which is asked for a solicitor and, without telling the client that the adviser is not a solicitor, provides an adviser who is not a solicitor, should not be entitled to recover anything ..."

When is a "fact" not a fact?

One thing I must warn you about is the illogical position the legal profession adopts when it comes to the subject of 'the facts' of a Judgment. Your Solicitor or Counsel will probably tell you that you cannot challenge a decision based on 'the facts'.

In other words, if a Judge has made a determination based on what they consider to be 'the facts', that's effectively it.

You only have grounds for an appeal if the Judge has interpreted 'the law' incorrectly. Facts don't seem to come into it.

But what if the Judge has got 'the facts' wrong?

What if the Judge has based their decision on matters which are not 'the facts'?

The real-world definition of a 'fact' is as follows:

FACT = "A thing that is known to be true"

However, in the legal world, if a Judge decides that something did (or did not) happen based on his or her incorrect understanding of what actually did happen, in the eyes of the legal profession, the Judge's determination is 'a fact' (whether it is true or not).

I have seen Judgments where Judges have made determinations based on things which were not true and made wild assumptions to fit the decision they wanted to give. If they had bothered to look at all the evidence it would not have supported their interpretation of the facts to be correct. They just chose to make their conclusions on matters which were not facts.

How can something be said to be 'a fact' when it is simply not true?

How can a Judgment be fair or credible if the information it is based on is incorrect?

You must prepare yourself for being told that the judiciary does not like to get involved in reviewing cases on the basis of 'the facts'. Once a Judge has made a decision, the determinations they make based on their interpretation of 'the facts' rarely seem to be questioned. In my opinion, that is a farce. I have never been given a logical or reasonable explanation from any practitioner in the legal profession which gives credibility to such a ludicrous stance.

Quite simply, if a Judge has determined something based on a fact which is not true, then any Judgment based on that interpretation must be flawed.

A fact is not a fact if it is not true. If 'a fact' in a Judgment can be proven to be untrue, then it surely cannot be said to be 'a fact'. Therefore, in my opinion, the judiciary should be able to review a case on 'the facts' if those facts can be demonstrated to be untrue. But don't hold your breath in the expectation that common sense and fair play will ever apply.

I bring this point to your attention because you should brace yourself before you discover the imperfections of the legal system and the frustration these may cause you.   As the old saying goes, the law really is an 'ass'.

In some circumstances, if it can be shown that the original Judge had no basis whatsoever for making findings of fact, an Appeal Court may intervene to overturn the finding/s. However, it is the role of the original Judge to decide which of the competing versions of the facts he or she prefers. Sometimes, mistakes do get made by Judges.

Appeal Courts usually take the view that the first Judge is the best person to reach a correct conclusion about the facts of the case (i.e. on the basis that the original Judge will have observed the witnesses giving evidence). Therefore, because the Appeal Court will only see a transcript of the evidence given by the witnesses, it is difficult for the Appeal Court to be able to disagree with the original trial Judge's finding of the facts (even if you know yourself that the original Judge was wrong). So, if the original Judge has made a 'balls up' of the facts of the case, it is like pushing a huge boulder up a hill when trying to overturn the decision.

You should also bear in mind that you cannot just appeal against a Judge's decision and have your case reconsidered before a higher Court. In order to seek an appeal, your legal team will have to apply for permission to appeal first, following the original Judgment. There is no guarantee that your case will be granted permission to appeal, yet alone get before an Appeal Court. The original Judge will probably have kept in mind the prospect of an appeal being made against his/her decision and will therefore have set out a version of the facts and his/her findings in such a way as to make obtaining permission to appeal difficult. So, just obtaining the permission to appeal is not a foregone conclusion and some cases will never even get that permission.

The reason for the Appeal Court not allowing cases to be reviewed on the facts is because they are overwhelmed. They go to great lengths to shut out appeals and an easy way of doing that is to say that a Judge's findings of fact cannot be challenged (even if you know those findings are complete bullsh*t) by the Appeal Court because the Judge supposedly had the benefit of seeing and hearing the witnesses. Trial Judges are acutely aware of this and therefore frame their

Judgments as 'findings of fact' which fit the law they have chosen to rely upon and the conclusions they have chosen to reach.

A Solicitor can move to another firm

A situation which you should prepare yourself for is one where your Solicitor moves to another firm mid-way through your case. I hope this does not happen to you – but it does happen quite frequently within the legal profession and when it does, it can be very disruptive to your case. One month your Solicitor is working for 'ABC Solicitors' and the next month he or she is off to 'XYZ Solicitors' and you don't know where you are.

Normally, the Solicitor working on your case will ask if you want to retain him or her when they go to the new firm. In that way, all the knowledge they have built up on your case will not be lost and they can continue with the minimum of disruption. In complex cases, most Clients prefer to keep their original Solicitor and so will move the case to the new firm with them. However, if your Solicitor moves to another firm, it can cause practical problems for you as a Client (even if you stay with the original firm and get another individual to take over the case or you move with your Solicitor to a new firm).

Why?

Because if you decide to stick with the original firm and have a new Solicitor take the case over, he or she will not necessarily have the same level of knowledge on the case. You may even find yourself being charged a fee for the replacement Solicitor to read themselves in to your file (although, that would be unreasonable and you should insist that any 'reading in' of the file is carried out free of charge).

If you decide to move to the new firm with your original Solicitor, then you may find yourself presented with a bill from the original firm to bring the account up to date. You will probably have to pay the bill before the original firm will release the files to the new firm where your Solicitor works. Without the files, your original Solicitor will probably be unable to do a thing with your case. You may find yourself in a situation where you are being asked for money just because your Solicitor has taken a personal decision to move firms (normally for their own self-interest). Had your Solicitor not moved firms, you may not have been required to pay any balancing bill because it would not have been issued until a later stage.

You may also find yourself losing the financial goodwill which you had built up with the original firm of Solicitors, which cannot be immediately replicated at the new firm. For example, you may have paid tens of thousands of pounds in fees to the original firm and that firm will appreciate the fact that you have paid so much to them. However, you may then be required to pay a sum of money into the account of the new firm, before they will allow your existing Solicitor to act!

Another problem you may face is that the new firm will not adopt the same approach on fees as your original firm did. For example, your old firm may have been flexible on when further payments were made but your new firm may not be. Your Solicitor may also not have as much influence on how such matters are dealt with at the new firm because he or she will be a 'new kid on the block'.

I mention the risk of your Solicitor moving firms mid-way through your case so you can prepare yourself for such an eventuality, should it occur. It can be highly detrimental to you. A degree of protection against this scenario happening to you is included in the 'Terms of Engagement' in Chapter 11.

Observations & Tips

- I say again, *never* praise your Solicitor or tell them they have done a good job (only do that at the end of the case if you have won). They are paid to do a good job for you. You won't necessarily know whether they have done a good job (or not) midway through your case. What can happen is, if you do praise them during the matter (however innocently), you can later discover that the job they have done is not as good as you were led to believe. If you ever have cause to take action against the Solicitor for negligence, they might try to say you were praising them during the case – inferring that you were somehow happy with the job they were doing.

- Remember, a litigation Solicitor's job is really all about managing 'uncertainty' in many cases. At the end of the day, that is all you will be getting in return for the fees they will charge you.

- In addition to the diary, also get yourself a notebook and record the amount of every bill you are sent. Keep a running total of how much you have spent and when you have paid. This may seem a really obvious tip but, believe me, costs can run away over time and you may be busy with your own job to notice. Your case could run for months or years and you'd be amazed at how the fees can accumulate. Also, use the book to keep a check on whether the fee estimates you have been given are accurate in reality.

- Some firms of Solicitors have monthly fee targets to hit. Watch out if they are billing you a set amount each month as part of the retainer.

- Keep a meticulous file yourself of all aspects of your case. Get a lever arch folder and put everything in date order so that you can look up anything you need to and refer to it. In obtaining the file notes your Solicitor makes, you can maintain a really detailed file – believe me, it will help in so many ways later on. You may end up knowing the file better than your Solicitor does, so when they need to find something they won't have to waste so much time locating it – you can tell them yourself. The other advantage to this is that, if you ever fall out with your Solicitor, you will have your own comprehensive file to give to another Solicitor, if needs be (because, invariably, unless you have paid your bills up to date, the Solicitor will not release your files and you can find yourself literally marooned).

- Don't get caught up in the emotion of your case and keep spending money on the chance that you might win. Sometimes, it's better to cut your losses and avoid larger costs at a later date. The Solicitor will get paid but you may lose your house!

- Sometimes the difference between winning and losing a case is just the party which gets tripped up first by some legal loophole or tactic identified or used by the other side.

- If your Solicitor or Counsel says your case is weak, it may be the best advice you ever get, despite how annoyed or disappointed you might feel. In the long run, you will save a great deal of money and stress by not pursuing it or settling.

- Being cross-examined in the witness box can be a traumatic and disturbing experience – mud can get thrown so you must be prepared for that. Your evidence can be twisted and taken completely out of context by the opposing Barrister, Q.C. or the Judge.

- Prepare yourself for the feeling you may have when you have stood in the witness box and told the truth but the Judge chooses not to believe you. You will feel outraged and helpless.

- Remember, when you've lost the shirt off your back after losing the case, your Solicitor probably isn't really going to lose much sleep over your personal circumstances – as long as they get their fees, they probably won't really give your situation a second thought.

- Be wary of situations arising where a Solicitor has committed you to the action and then keeps running up the fees but then stops working for you because you have run out of money. If this happens then the professional communication of your Solicitor must have gone seriously wrong.

- Always check the facts and details of the Particulars of Claim (or your Defence) and Witness Statement you will be asked to sign. Although it may be drafted by your Counsel or Solicitor, you may assume that it's correct and sign it in good faith. DON'T! If they have misunderstood anything and put it in writing, they will probably blame you. The same goes for the Pre-action Protocol Letter.

- At the start, take time to obtain the SRA Code of Conduct or the relevant Law Society Practice Rules and keep them to hand. They are an invaluable source of reference. You can do this by contacting The Law Society in your region (see Chapter 10 for contact details).

- If you have a disagreement or an issue over something which your Solicitor has done (or not done) and you are mid-way through your case, then a good idea is to tell them the issues you have but reserve the right to dispute the bill when it is drawn up later. For example, a Solicitor may have failed to act on something which means that your opponent makes an application to the Court to have your case thrown out, or the like. In order to bring your case back on track you may have to make a counter-application to the Court which all costs money. If this was avoidable, then you have every right to complain and refuse to pay the cost for your Solicitor's failure to act. Reserving the right to dispute the extra costs at a later date means that you can (hopefully) avoid falling out with your Solicitor and concentrate on taking your case forward.

- Occasionally, Solicitors move to other law firms mid-way through people's cases. This can prove to be an unwelcome disruption to your case. Normally, a Solicitor will take your case with them to the new firm - because they know it better than anyone else. However, be aware that you can find yourself in a situation where the new firm has a different company culture (i.e. towards fee payments or arrangements which you had with the previous firm are no longer continued). Your Solicitor will also be a "new kid on the block" at the new firm and possibly won't be able to influence matters in the same way they did at the old firm. You must therefore inform your Solicitor of your requirements if such a move occurs. A suggestion to help you is included in the 'Terms of Engagement' in Chapter 11.

- As the trial approaches things can get stressful. Costs can be more than you had expected, witness statement exchanges and disclosure can be frustrating and you might get fed up because the positive advice you had originally received may turn into less positive on account of your Solicitor's insecurities.

- Be prepared for the fact that you may get a Judge who does not understand your case or the field you need them to. It's a lottery as to whether you get a Judge capable of properly assessing a situation.

- Be prepared for a Judge to say things in his or her Judgment which do not have any basis in fact and use them to form their conclusions and findings. Remember, Judges are human and do not always get it right.

- Be prepared to be told by your legal team that you can't appeal a decision on the facts. Be prepared for being told you can only appeal on points of law.

- Your Solicitor may tell you that if the case does not go in your favour then you can appeal the decision (i.e. you may be given the impression that there is a second chance to see justice prevail). Certainly, if your case needs to be appealed then the option should be available. However, do not automatically assume that the Court will allow the case to be appealed. That is why it is essential that your legal team do what they are paid for well – nailing all the points of trial.

- Never try to second guess or speculate what the Judge is thinking at trial. It will drive you mad and there is no guarantee that you will be right. Use your energy elsewhere.

- Remember that resolving legal issues can take a long time. What starts out as a seemingly simple issue with an opponent can take months or even years to conclude.

- Bear in mind that the truthful and honest party does not always win. The bad guys do get away with it sometimes.

- When you go and see your Solicitor, most of us walk blindly into the situation and give ourselves over to him or her because they are supposed to know what they are doing. However, be prepared to be deflated when it all goes wrong and for your Solicitor to blame you for following the advice they gave you!

- If you find yourself in a situation where you are without the services of a Solicitor and you need legal assistance but cannot afford to pay for it, you can get in touch with the '**LawWorks**' organisation. This is a charitable operation which helps to find free legal assistance from volunteer Solicitors. Assistance from 'LawWorks' is available to those who cannot afford to pay legal fees and cannot obtain public funding (Legal Aid). You will need to apply to 'LawWorks' either through an Advice Agency (i.e. Citizen's Advice Bureau or Law Centre). Further details can be found at **_www.lawworks.org.uk_** or at **LawWorks (Solicitors' Pro Bono Group)**, The National Pro Bono Centre, 48 Chancery Lane, London WC2A 1JF. Telephone 0207 092 3940. Guidance on finding advice agencies is contained on their website. The application can also be downloaded from the website. **PLEASE BEAR IN MIND IT IS A CHARITABLE ORGANISATION AND HAS LIMITED RESOURCES. THE WORK WHICH IT CARRIES OUT IS INVALUABLE TO THE PEOPLE IT HELPS. THE ORGANISATION IS GRATEFUL FOR CHARITABLE DONATIONS.** Assistance with finding a Solicitor (and finding out whether you are eligible for Legal Aid) is also available via the **Community Legal Advice Service** on 0845 345 4 345 (or _www.communitylegaladvice.org.uk_).

CHAPTER 5

The Importance of the Cost Estimate

Despite what anyone may say about the merits of taking legal action, it is the 'COST' of taking the action which is a critical factor for people deciding whether to proceed with the action or not.

What is the point of spending huge sums of money when the potential return will not justify it?

What is the point of starting an action and you later discover that the costs are higher than you were originally told and you can't afford to continue?

The 'Costs Information' is the most important element of the advice given to you by a Solicitor. The 'cost estimate' is the *barometer* by which you can measure the sense in taking the action and the extent to which you are prepared to put up with the resultant stress, frustration and nausea of the case itself.

This is also backed up by the words of Lord Justice Dyson in the case of ***Leigh v Michelin Tyre PLC [2003] EWCA Civ 1766*** where he said in paragraph 22 about the purpose of a cost estimate:

> "....it is to enable all parties to the litigation to know what their potential liability for costs may be. That enables them to decide whether to attempt to settle the litigation, or to pursue it and (in the latter case) what resources to apply to the litigation ......"

In practice, you may find that some Solicitors are very reluctant to give you an overall costs estimate at the outset when you come to them for advice. They may say:

"We can't give you an estimate yet because we don't know what's involved"

or

"All we can do is tell you what it will cost to get to the next stage".

Well, those excuses are **total bunk**.

I would advise you to stop using any Solicitor who relies on such excuses to avoid giving you an overall estimate of costs.

The fact is that, if your Solicitor is experienced in the field you need them to be, then he or she should be able to give you an overall estimate of costs **within a range of possible outcomes** at the beginning (or certainly before committing you to spending thousands of pounds of your hard earned money).

Of course, you cannot expect a Solicitor to be able to give you an overall estimate which is accurate down to the nearest penny at the outset. That would be unrealistic. However, all you are asking them to do is to give you a series of 'ball-park' global figures at the earliest opportunity. That is an entirely reasonable request to make of your Solicitor. Only after that will you be able to put any estimate 'to get your case to the next stage' into perspective. That's the way round it should work. Without a 'global' estimate any other estimate is meaningless. A *detailed* estimate for the overall costs should follow not long afterwards though.

A word of warning! A Solicitor may give you a vague estimate of costs along the lines of *"oh, it may cost five figures"* or in some cases they may say *"oh, it may cost six figures"*. Again, that is not acceptable. You see, there is a massive difference between £10,000 and £99,000 – those are both five figure sums. There is an enormous difference between £100,000 and £999,000 – those are both six figure sums. When someone says five figures, most people assume a figure of £10,000 and this sum may seem affordable. However, when you then get a bill for £99,000 at the end, that sum is nothing like the £10,000 you were originally led to believe the case may cost. The same principle can be applied to the six figure argument where £999,000 is way in excess of £100,000. I am sure you get my point – so please do not let a Solicitor get away with giving you a lazy attempt at an estimate in those circumstances.

I feel that it is relevant to mention at this stage of the advice giving process, that some Solicitors may be looking at your case as a potential piece of business for their firm (i.e. where there is money to be made – bear in mind also that some firms even set monthly fee-targets for their Solicitors to achieve). Accordingly, they might be hesitant to give you an estimate which is too high in case they frighten you away. I can say this because a Solicitor told me this is a dilemma that he faces frequently. However, although it may be a human tendency in the commercial world in which we live today, that is no excuse for a Solicitor to ignore your request or lack the courage to tell you the reality.

Think of it like this: you wouldn't sign up to buy a car if the salesperson hasn't told you how much it would cost, would you? You wouldn't allow yourself to be committed to buying that car on the strength of the salesperson saying "*I can't tell you exactly how much it would cost because I don't know what extras you want – but I will commit you to buying it by telling you how much one wheel costs or the door mirror*". It would be absurd.

OK, the car example may not appeal to some of you. You could use a different analogy of a builder giving a quote for an extension to your house – but the point is the same. Unless you've got more money than sense, you wouldn't just sign a blank cheque to your Solicitor without knowing what you are potentially in for.

I once met a Solicitor who was Head of Litigation at a medium sized firm of London Solicitors. I asked him if he gave Clients an overall fee estimate at the outset of their case. He looked at me disbelievingly and said "*we don't do that – we don't have a crystal ball – we wouldn't know how much it would cost*".

I was astonished and asked him this question in response:

"*OK then, if you are the expert with all the experience in litigation, and you don't know how much something might cost, how can you expect a 'lay-person' Client to know?*"

And.......

"If the Client doesn't have an idea about the costs, then how are they supposed to be able to decide whether or not they wish to proceed with the action?"

The man looked at me blankly and shrugged his shoulders. He gave me no answer. I am afraid that his attitude is all too common in my experience with some Solicitors – they expect the Client to have a crystal ball! Be aware that there are some Solicitors out there who treat Clients as if they are on this planet for their own convenience. These Solicitors will quite happily commit a Client to an action without properly informing them on costs and risks (or only attempting to do so when it is too late and the Client has progressed too far with the action to stop). That's sheer arrogance, in my opinion. The man also later admitted that he didn't know what the SRA Codes were and said he would have to go back and look them up!

A Solicitor is obligated under SRA/Law Society rules to provide you with the **'best information possible about the likely overall cost of a matter at the outset and, where appropriate, as the matter progresses'.**

Compulsory Costs Budgeting

As mentioned earlier, a regime called 'Costs Budgeting' has been in force since April 2013 for Lawyers acting for parties in litigation. 'Costs Budgeting' is a compulsory element of the service provided to Clients.

Prior to 2013, it had been common for parties in a dispute to find themselves in situations where the costs were the driving factor in the litigation - rather than the Solicitor and Counsel focusing on providing legal advice on the merits of a claim. In many cases, the total legal fees for all parties often exceeded the basic sums in dispute.

The fundamental principle of 'Costs Budgeting' is that the power to manage the costs in a litigation case is given to the Court under the existing case management powers it has. When a claim is lodged in Court, the Court will then issue a notice of how the case will be allocated in the Court system and it will set a deadline for the filing of a 'Costs Budget' for both sides. Active costs management is now carried out by the Court and this is broadly done as follows:

1. Each party's Solicitor prepares a 'Costs Budget' soon after the case is lodged in Court (i.e. after the 'Allocation Questionnaire'/'Directions Questionnaire' is completed). The Court will issue a notice of a proposed case allocation and it will set a deadline for filing the costs budgets for both sides.

2. The Court will then consider and approve each party's budget, with revisions where appropriate. A 'Costs Budget' will be agreed and established between all parties. The 'Costs Budget' can then be updated and amended as the case proceeds, if necessary. A 'Costs Management Conference' may be necessary if amendments need to be made at a later date.

   [When the 'Costs Budgets' have been filed and exchanged, the Court will make a 'Costs Management Order' unless it is satisfied that the litigation can be conducted justly and at a proportionate cost without such an order being made. Once a 'Costs Management Order' has been made, it will be very difficult for any party to deviate from the budget].

3. The Court will then manage the case on the basis that the case will progress in accordance with the approved costs budgets.

4. In theory, the costs recoverable by the successful party would be assessed at the end of the proceedings by reference to the agreed 'Costs Budget' (i.e. the parties should stick to the agreed budget or suffer consequences if the budget is exceeded unnecessarily). If there is a difference of more than 20% in the final bill, an explanation will need to be made to the Court by the receiving party.

Usually, the first time a Court will be able to consider the parties' costs is at the initial 'Case Management Conference'. This gives the Court the opportunity to review the progress of the dispute in general and set a timetable for the parties to follow in the lead up to the trial.

Keeping costs in proportion

Costs in the 'Costs Budget' must be proportionate to the matters in hand on the case. In theory, costs will be deemed to be proportionate if they bear a reasonable relationship to:

- the value of any *non-monetary* relief being sought in the claim
- the complexity of the litigation
- any additional work generated by the conduct of the parties
- any other factors associated with the proceedings (i.e. reputation and public importance)

So, in theory, the parties in a litigation matter should *not* see themselves in a situation where they spend more than a proportionate amount of money when bringing or defending a claim. If parties do wish to spend more, they will be able to do so (in most cases). However, under the 'Costs Budgeting' regime, the party should not expect to receive such sums from the other party.

In effect, the 'Costs Budget' disclosed and agreed by each party should be as good as a guarantee that the fees will be adhered to. The 'Costs Budget' will be looked upon as if it is a detailed assessment of the costs in a 'loser pays winner' situation. However, the 'Costs Budget' will not necessarily be used as a tool for detailed assessment of costs paid by a Client to their own Solicitor.

The Court will not generally deviate from the approved budget without good reason.

Accordingly, your Solicitor will need to advise you properly on the costs and you should have the opportunity to review and approve the budgets before they are exchanged with the opposing party and proceed to Court if desired. In addition,

'Costs Budgets' will contain costs for specified matters which should enable you to budget and forecast future expenditure. You might also consider it necessary to attend Court hearings at which 'Cost Budgets' are discussed and agreed.

Costs Budgeting - is it a perfect solution?

'Costs Budgeting' is a welcome measure to inform Clients about the total cost of the case. However, it still has some shortcomings. The potential problems with the 'Costs Budgeting' regime are set out as follows:

- If the original 'Costs Budget' has not been done properly (i.e. because the Solicitor has overlooked what they claim to be an unexpected future cost which results in the budget being increased by the Court at a later stage), the Client will have been denied the opportunity to make an informed decision at an earlier stage about whether they wish to continue with the case to trial or not. The Client could potentially be liable for costs which they were not expecting.

- After the original 'Costs Budget' is approved, a party could make an application to have the budget amended at a 'Costs Management Conference'. If there are any delays in being able to arrange such a conference, further costs could be incurred which the Client was originally unaware of.

- The 'Costs Budget' does not contain all of the potential costs a party may face as a consequence of the entire litigation process. For example, it does not set out what the potential costs might be if one party wishes to appeal the outcome of the trial. It also does not set out what the potential costs might be if a party wishes to have the final costs assessed by a Costs Judge.

- Most significantly though, the 'Costs Budget' process fails to address the 'advance' costs advice gap between the time period from when a Solicitor takes on a case to when the claim and 'Costs Budget' are eventually lodged in the Court. For example, a Solicitor may take several months (or more) to assess and work on the case, gathering evidence and advice from Counsel and educating themselves in the background facts of the matter before the claim is lodged in Court. This can take a considerable period of time and expense. Believe me, this does happen!

Therefore, it is vitally important for the Solicitor to give the Client proper advice on all aspects of the potential costs well in advance of the completion of the claim and questionnaire. Otherwise, a Client can find themselves in a situation where the Solicitor has run up considerable costs before the claim is lodged in Court and only then finds out what the whole action might realistically cost.

Estimates being exceeded

Even with the 'Costs Budgeting' regime in force, there is still a risk that cost estimates can be exceeded as your case progresses. Also, you have to factor in all of the costs incurred by your opponent into the equation (which can also increase and which you have little or no control over yourself). Also, don't forget the additional costs of an appeal should you lose the case as a result of a perverse decision made by a Judge!

So, how do you protect yourself from potentially misleading and incomplete cost information?

How do you protect yourself from being put in a position where your Solicitor has run up such high costs (which you weren't expecting) which you can't afford to pay and you then wish you had never started the action?

The 'TCF' Principle for Cost Estimates

There is no doubt that the 'Costs Budgeting' process is a helpful measure - but it is not perfect. However, you should not just rely on this process to provide you with meaningful advanced costs information. In order to assist you further, I have devised a formula for you to use which will help prepare and protect yourself. For the purposes of this book, call it the **'TCF'** for cost estimates and, if you use it, you shouldn't go far wrong. TCF stands for the '**True Cost Formula**'.

This formula will help you avoid falling victim to a Solicitor who lacks the courage to tell you the true overall costs at the outset of your case. It works like this:

Say your Solicitor tells you that your costs in the case will be £20,000 (that's a relatively cheap case on average, by the way, in England).

Take that £20,000 and multiply it by x 1.5. This will give you what I call the 'Probable' figure.

Then take the £20,000 and multiply it by x 2. This will give you the 'Possible' figure (a worst case scenario).

Now factor in your opponent's costs which your Solicitor has told you are £18,000.

Do the same with that £18,000 figure to get the 'Probable' and 'Possible' figures.

Now add the cost of any appeal should you lose the case (say £10,000 in this example – to cover your costs and your opponent's).

You will then have a better idea of what the cost implications are and what you need to prepare for.

I summarise this in the table below:

The TCF Principle

(Based on an estimate of £20,000 for your own costs)

	Estimate	'Probable' (x1.5)	'Possible' (x2)
Your costs:	£20,000	£30,000	£40,000
Opponents costs:	£18,000	£27,000	£36,000
	£38,000	£57,000	£76,000
Appeal costs:	£10,000	£15,000	£20,000

Overall costs: **£48,000**   **£72,000**   **£96,000**

You may think at first glance that this formula is unrealistic. I can assure you that it is *not*. In my experience (and in the experience of other people I have consulted), this formula is highly realistic. It really spells out what can happen. Whilst you would hope that the estimate of costs provided by your Solicitor is the accurate one, the costs under the 'Probable' column are those which can quite easily be realised. Therefore, expect something between 'Estimate' and 'Probable'. Use the 'Possible' figure as a worst case scenario.

In other words, on a £20,000 case the cost to you if you lose could be £72,000 or more on the 'Probable' basis alone!

Just imagine the costs for a £50,000 case (on the 'probable' scale alone they could reach £180,000 overall if you lost). Many cases which go to the High Court in London can last for 5 to 7 days for example are usually estimated to cost six figure sums and can run into £500,000+ at the end when all party's costs are combined. These are enormous sums of money.

To give you an example of a case where the Client has been told that their costs are £500,000, this would translate as follows:

(Based on an estimate of £500,000 for your own costs)

	Estimate	'Probable' (x1.5)	'Possible' (x2)
Your costs:	£500,000	£750,000	£1,000,000
Opponents costs:	£480,000	£720,000	£960,000
	£980,000	£1,470,000	£1,960,000
Appeal costs:	£200,000	£300,000	£400,000
Overall costs:	**£1,180,000**	**£1,770,000**	**£2,360,000**

I cannot stress the importance of knowing the potential costs of your case and how they can run away. You must insist that your Solicitor gives you an overall estimate of the outset, even if the figure is a deliberate over-estimate. Better to plan for too much than too little, especially if you find yourself wishing to have the bills assessed in Court because that will mean further expense (see Chapter 9).

Finally, do not forget to add VAT on top of the costs!

ASK YOUR SOLICITOR TO PROVIDE YOU WITH THESE ESTIMATES OF COSTS AT THE OUTSET OF YOUR RETAINER.

<u>**Be wary of the 'interim' bill argument to justify overall fees charged**</u>

Watch out for reasons given by some Solicitors to defend their high fee charges when they have not provided a full overall estimate. Having heard about several legal cases, not just my father's, there seems to be a presumption amongst some Solicitors that Clients must know what the total fees are going to eventually be just because the Solicitor sends a series of bills without giving a prior overall estimate.

Time and time again there have been cases where a Solicitor has attempted to use the argument to justify their fees along the lines of *"well, the Client must have been aware of the overall costs because we sent him interim bills"*. This is a ridiculous defence against high charges and one which completely flies in the face of the regulatory requirements governing advance costs information for Clients. Using such an argument is rather like me saying that you must know the value of my uncle's house because I've told you how much it cost to replace his windows! You need to be given an overall estimate at the outset and without it you will have no means of knowing what you are potentially in for.

<u>**The Cost Risk Benefit Analysis**</u>

It's a phrase you will hear throughout this book. The level of cost should always be considered in relation to the overall 'risks' of your action and 'benefit' it may bring (or may not) at the end of your case. There is absolutely no point in paying out huge sums of money if the return is not going to give you more than you have paid. Equally, the risk of your action is critical and you should expect your

Solicitor to give you an opinion on risk expressed in percentage terms (i.e. *"your case has a 70% chance of success"*).

If your Solicitor says you only have a 50% chance of success then, in my opinion, it means they haven't got a clue what the outcome might be. If they maintain that 50% is the chance you have got then it is questionable if your risk will justify the potentially costly legal action – but the decision will be up to you.

You may find that you have to spend some money to allow your Solicitor to reach a stage where they can give you an informed opinion on the percentage chance of success (which in complex cases may also involve the services of a Barrister or Q.C.) – but don't allow them to go too far. Ideally, you would expect a Solicitor to be able to give you advice on costs, risks and benefits *before* he or she issues your claim officially in the Court and commits you to the action.

For your information, you should keep in mind the case of **Holmes v National Benzole Co (1968) 109 SJ 971** where Justice Lyell said:

> "A solicitor who, without any investigation of his client's claim, allowed or encouraged a client to pursue a claim which proper investigation would at an early stage have shown to be a hopeless one was in breach of duty to his client."

The above quotation enforces the argument that a Solicitor is required to properly assess a Client's case and investigate costs, risks and benefits as well as advise on other crucial aspects at the earliest possible stage of the case. If a Solicitor does not carry these out for a Client and the case turns out to be a hopeless one, then he or she has simply not done their job. The Solicitor will therefore be in breach of their professional obligation to the Client.

Certainly, the 'Costs Budgeting' process should make life easier for a Client to a certain extent (and many of these issues may not arise). However, one possible positive consequence of the exchange of 'Costs Budgets' by each party is that, once confronted with the financial figures in black-and-white for both sets of costs, parties may become disinclined to continue with the case because they can see how much it will cost if they lose. Consequently, the parties will be more inclined to explore alternative means of resolving the dispute in order to avoid the worst case outcome.

Mediation

An alternative (and less costly) way of dealing with a legal case is to seek mediation between the parties at the earliest possible stage. The purpose of this is to settle a case without a Court trial. In fact, Courts tend to encourage all disputes to be resolved by an alternative means such as this in order to avoid full blown trials. If your case can be resolved by mediation, then I would urge you to do everything you can in order to achieve settlement by that route.

How should you approach the subject of taking Legal Action or defending it?

If you have no financial constraints then the answer is that it doesn't matter! However, for most of us the opposite is true. Many people approach the idea of taking legal action by saying to themselves:

How much will I get if I win?

That's fine for some, especially if money is no object. It's not necessarily the wrong approach for anyone else either. However, from personal experience, it is far more sensible to approach taking legal action by saying to yourself:

How much will it cost me if I lose?

You may recall when I mentioned earlier that many people who have taken legal action in the past would dearly love to be able to turn the clock back and never have spent their money on it. Don't be one of these people!

What information is a Solicitor required to provide on costs?

A Solicitor must:

- Give you the best information possible about the likely overall costs.

- Explain to you the likely time to be spent (especially if it is relevant to the calculation of fees).

- Give you the best information possible by either:

- Agreeing a fixed fee
- Giving a realistic overall estimate
- Giving a forecast within a range of potential costs
- Explaining why it is not possible to provide the above three points and instead give you the best information possible about costs of the next stage of the matter

- Explain your right to set an upper limit on fees.

- Clarify at the outset between whether the costs information is an 'estimate' or a 'quotation' and ensure you understand the difference.

- Explain to you how the fees are calculated.

- Inform you if charging rates ever get increased.

- Tell you how the firm will charge you if the matter is not completed.

- Explain to you what foreseeable payments you will need to make to any party and when these will need to be made.

- Agree with you times or stages when you will be updated on costs information (including not only your costs incurred but also advising when a costs estimate or limit may be exceeded). A Solicitor should also advise on any change in circumstances which affect your potential liability for costs, risks or cost-benefit position.

- Explain to you the firm's billing arrangements.

- Explore the availability of alternative funding arrangements.

- Advise you on the cost/risk/benefit analysis of pursuing your action.

- Disclose to you any relevant arrangement which a Solicitor has with a third party (such as a lender, fee-sharer or an introducer which may affect you or your Solicitor's conduct of the matter).

- Advise you if the firm requires money to be paid to it 'on account'.

If you are a publicly funded Client (i.e. using Legal Aid), the Solicitor must:

- Explain your potential liability for your own costs and those of any other party, such as:

- The effect of the charges and their likely amount
- The obligation to pay any contribution (and the consequences of failure to do so)
- The fact that you may still be ordered by the Court to contribute to your opponent's cost if the case is lost, even though your own costs are publicly funded
- The risk of your opponent not being ordered or able to pay costs, even if you win

If you are a privately-paying Client in a litigation matter (i.e. where the parties in any action are at odds with each other), the Solicitor must:

- Explain to you your potential liability for your own costs and those of any other party, such as:

- The fact that you will be responsible for paying the firm's bill in full, regardless of any order for costs made against your opponent

- The potential liability for your opponent's costs as well as your own costs, if the case is lost
- The risk of your opponent not being ordered (or able) to pay your costs
- The implications of your opponents being legally aided
- The possible cost implications of you rejecting the option to settle your case via mediation (or an alternative means of dispute resolution)
- The costs and risks of having to enforce Judgments (i.e. further action you may need to take – or have taken against you – after the case is finished)
- The cost implications if you withdraw or reject a reasonable offer for settlement from your opponent

PLEASE NOTE THAT THE ABOVE INFORMATION IS MERELY PROVIDED TO DEMONSTRATE THE MAIN POINTS OF IMPORTANCE (THE LIST IS NOT EXHAUSTIVE).

The need for a Solicitor to be a business person

Clients often only find out about the *true* costs, risks, inconvenience and stress caused by litigation when it's too late.

What a Client needs at the outset is to be told (in the bluntest terms) what the costs and risks may be and the potential stress the legal action may cause.

If a Solicitor follows very basic principles when giving advice to Clients in the early stages, then many Clients will probably not allow themselves to be drawn into litigation. If the Client is determined to proceed, then they can do so with their 'eyes wide open' in the full knowledge of the potential costs and risks.

Taking (or defending) legal action is no different from any other business venture or project an individual may embark upon.

A Client needs to be able to plan and budget for it and then to be able to put a 'business plan' together for the case. If a businessman were to embark on a business project where the costs and risks were unknown (or had not been properly evaluated), he would end up on the fast-track to failure and ultimate disappointment.

Unfortunately, many litigation Solicitors are not all-round business people – but they should be! Sadly, in my experience from those I have come into contact with (and from speaking to other people who have been involved in litigation), many Solicitors do not seem to fully appreciate the importance of giving meaningful 'upfront' advice on potential costs and risks which enable a Client to plan.

I hope this chapter will go some way to addressing that problem and make some Solicitors realise that litigation is not all about them trying to justify their fees and advice after the 'horse has bolted from the stable' when it's too late for the Client.

A Solicitor should not let that 'horse out of that stable' unless the Client has been told exactly where that horse may go – and told the costs and risks of it getting there.

Observations & Tips

- Insist that your Solicitor gives you an overall estimate of costs at the outset, even if they are not accurate to the nearest penny.

- Expect your Solicitor to be able to give you a series of estimates across a range of possible outcomes. Ask them to do this based on their experience of cases like yours.

- If your Solicitor says they can't do it then you must question if they actually have the requisite experience to be dealing with your case.

- Remember that it's not just your own costs you have to plan for. Always consider the cost of your opponents and the expense of an appeal (plus the costs of having the bills assessed if you lose).

- Remember, costs can run away when work gets going on your case – use *The TCF Principle* to inform yourself of the potential costs involved.

- <u>Never</u> just approach the case on the basis of 'How much will I get if I win?'

- <u>Always</u> approach the case on the basis of **'How much will it cost me if I lose?'**

- Insist that your Solicitor gives you a cost/risk/benefit analysis of your case before committing you to any action.

- Insist that all advice on costs is followed up in writing by your Solicitor.

- Are you being charged the correct rate for the grade of fee earner on your case?

- Keep that special notebook (or file) specifically for the purpose of recording invoices sent. Keep a running total of the amount of fees you have paid. This may seem an obvious tip – but you wouldn't believe how many people don't do it. You will be surprised at how the fees mount up. Update your records as soon as you receive a bill or pay it.

- Always check each bill when you receive it. The breakdown/explanation of what has been charged needs to be compliant with rules. You should not be charged for photocopying and petty incidentals (i.e. non-essentials). The bills must also be signed by a partner at the firm to comply with the law. Also, ask for the time-sheets recording the work done. These should correspond with the bill.

- *Never* accept an explanation from your Solicitor that because you were sent bills by the firm as the case progressed, you must have known how much the case was going to cost overall. That is no excuse for not providing you with an overall estimate.

- Make sure you're not being charged fees for work done by inexperienced people at the firm (i.e. your Solicitor may quote you an hourly rate for themselves but then go on to use a team of people – in reality, the hourly rate quoted will be inaccurate because it will increase on account of more people being involved).

- Question the experience of everyone in a team (i.e. what are they bringing to your case that is worth paying for?).

- For a profession which likes to portray its worth through Solicitors' sophistication and expertise, bear in mind that there sure isn't much of it when it comes to giving meaningful and accurate fee quotes. There seems to be nothing sophisticated about fee quotes at all.

- Solicitors lead a very privileged existence whereby they just bill you for time spent on a matter, even if it has not benefited you. For most of us, we don't enjoy such a charmed existence because we only get paid a set salary or when we get results. That is why it is essential that you receive an acceptable level of service from your Solicitor and that means proper estimates on costs.

- Bear in mind that many people suffer miscarriages of justice and find themselves in a position where they have a good cause to appeal. However, they cannot always afford to take the matter further to seek justice. Money is what really matters and that's why it is essential that you are given the full picture on potential costs by your Solicitor.

- Always take steps to establish if the opponent in your case can afford to pay you if you win. Many a case has been won but the result is worthless if the winner never receives any money.

- If they say your case has a *60% chance of success*, be extremely cautious when weighing up the pros and cons of your action. In my opinion, when they say that your case has a 60% chance of success, they don't actually feel absolutely confident it can be won. To my mind, it may mean they just fancy having a go at it for you (as long as you are going to pay them for giving them the privilege of the opportunity). Obviously, 60% sounds better than 50%. However, it is their way of drawing you in to the action by making you think that you are more likely to win than lose. I can say this because other people I have spoken to who were told their cases had a 60% chance of success, feel exactly the same as me. Some either lost their cases or pulled out of them. Be very wary of that! You should only start to be more comforted when your Solicitor (or Counsel) tells you that your case has at least a 70% chance of success. But that's not even a guaranteed outcome – so please be warned.

CHAPTER 6

The Importance of Insurance for Your Case

You may be surprised at me telling you about insurance in this book – if not, merely for the fact that insurance exists for legal cases. I can say it was certainly a revelation to me when I found out that such a vehicle existed to help Clients in litigation!

Well, the reason I want to mention it is because it is an important factor in the whole approach to the litigation. It is also a factor which my father was never advised about by the firm of Solicitors he used. The firm was completely ignorant of the existence of insurance for him (and probably their other Clients too).

Quite simply, if my father had been advised about the option of having his case insured, he would never have proceeded with the action. I say this because his case was prepared so badly that no insurer would have taken the risk of insuring it. Thus, it would have revealed the incomplete advice he had received from his firm of Solicitors at an early stage of the proceedings to enable him to pull out.

"After-the-Event" Insurance

I have already mentioned that it is a professional obligation for a Solicitor to advise you on the availability of insurance for your case. This insurance is designed to cover the costs of your case in the event that you lose. This is commonly referred to as 'after-the-event' insurance.

Your Solicitor is not only responsible for advising you about this crucial option, but your Solicitor is also responsible for arranging the policy with the insurer (or a specialist broker). The premise of the insurance is that you can more easily afford to take the legal action and lose. Obviously, an insurer will look to insure cases which it feels are going to be won, but that is their choice. From your perspective, it is there to fall back on in the event that you lose.

An additional and practical advantage in having after-the-event insurance is that it can send a strong message to your opponent in the case. If your opponent is made aware that you have insurance in place it can sometimes make them see sense (or abandon the action) before it gets to Court – because they realise the chances of the case going all the way are high but you won't be bothered about the cost. In my opinion, that is why it is essential that your Solicitor seeks to obtain the insurance for you at the earliest possible stage in order to increase the chances of your case being settled at the earliest opportunity, without any further unnecessary financial outlay.

Specialist lending organisations

Amazingly (well it was to a lay-person like me when I discovered it), it is sometimes possible to find specialist lenders who will put up the money for you to fund your case if you have an 'after-the-event' insurance policy in place. The lender takes security from the insurance policy in return for loaning the money.

You will pay interest on the loan but the idea is that it enables you to pay out less money and plan your cash flow accordingly. In theory therefore, if you have a good case it should be possible to go to Court and it will cost you virtually nothing (by comparison to having to fund it yourself). If you lose, you will have to pay the premium for the insurance policy – but that's usually nowhere near the total cost of the action itself. Some insurers do not even require the premium to be paid on the policy until after the case has ended.

I should stress caution before you get too excited about insurance and finding a lender to put up the money for your case. Both organisations will have certain criteria which need to be met and there is no guarantee that you will obtain funding from a lender. The same can be said for the insurers themselves. However, if an insurer is not willing to insure your case because it does not like the risk, then why should you take the risk with the case yourself?

With caution comes a stark reality-check!

Cost/Risk/Benefit Analysis

You won't be surprised to learn that 'cost/risk/benefit analysis' is crucial for any potential insurer when looking at covering you on your case. The insurer will want to see a detailed analysis of the potential costs and the risks expressed as a percentage. This means that your Solicitor and Barrister or Q.C. will have to put this information together for presentation to the insurer.

I state that the insurer's insistence on such detailed information is still beneficial to you – even if they turn your insurance down.

Why?

Because it means that you will see for yourself what the cost/risk/benefit analysis is so you can decide whether you wish to proceed with your action. I cannot stress the value of that enough to anyone.

Inadequate advice on insurance by a Solicitor

You are now aware that a Solicitor is professionally obliged to discuss the prospect of having your case insured. However, you may find that some Solicitors try to cover themselves by just mentioning the phrase 'insurance' in their Terms of Business or Client Care letter.

A Solicitor might use the phrase *"we will discuss with you the subject of insurance and whether the cost of your case may be covered by an insurance policy you already have........"*

What they are referring to here is the possibility that you may already have a separate 'pre-paid' insurance policy (such as legal expenses cover through membership of a trade body or on your household insurance policy) which may cover your costs. These policies are also known as 'before-the-event' arrangements.

The reliance on such policies is *not* acceptable as far as a Solicitor meeting his obligation to explore the subject of insurance for you.

A Solicitor who adopts that approach really does not understand what insurance is or their own professional obligations to a Client.

It is quite unusual in the insurance industry to find an insurer providing a 'bolt-on' cover to a separate policy which covers costs of taking legal action. Only some household insurance plans may have legal expenses cover and it will probably only provide cover for specific situations. Also, where you do have separate legal expenses plans (either attached to your public/employers liability insurance for your business or your household contents/buildings insurance) these might only be designed to cover the costs of *defending* an action against you (and only up to certain monetary limits). For example, you may find that you have cover attached to your business employer's liability insurance but it will generally only cover you for a defence of legal action from an employee over an employment issue or a defence of an action over a tax issue. Similar restrictions will apply to any household policy which includes legal expenses cover.

What I am saying is that these types of insurance plans may just be 'defence only' policies and may not cover your action. Just imagine that you are an insurance company and you say that you will cover the cost of legal action which anyone wishes to take as part of the cover bolted on to a household policy. You would be out of business within a week!

In some cases you may find a policy which provides legal expenses cover (such as special policies for Landlords to protect themselves and their property against the actions of Tenants or household or business policies where legal expenses cover has been included) but in the main, it is unlikely that the average person will have such a policy.

You should always check with your household or business insurer to see if you have cover for legal expenses. In that way, you will know for sure!

It is therefore not acceptable for a Solicitor to suggest they have covered the insurance aspect on the basis of merely mentioning existing insurance policies you may have.

Some household insurance policies do cover legal expenses for non-business issues. Some business insurance policies also cover legal expenses for non-business issues. Use of these policies should always be investigated, although such policies often limit the policyholder to using a Solicitor from an insurer's own panel who might not be competent or expert in the field required and the insurers are typically 'tight-fisted' and unreasonable.

I feel it is worthwhile mentioning the subject of 'CONTINGENCY fee arrangements' and 'CONDITIONAL fee arrangements' in this chapter, if only to demonstrate that they are not strictly insurance in the same sense as the 'after-the-event' policies – but they are an alternative means of enabling you to avoid or reduce the payment of legal fees.

Conditional Fee Arrangements (CFA's)

A 'Conditional Fee Arrangement' (CFA) is a different type of arrangement where payment to a Solicitor is still dependent upon the result of the proceedings.

A CFA is an agreement where a Solicitor/Lawyer and the Client agree to share the risks of litigation by coming to an arrangement on the fees payable on the result of the litigation.

There are 2 types of CFA:

1. A 'No Win, No Fee' arrangement. In the event of losing, the Client will not be liable to pay any fees to their Lawyer. If the case is won, fees are payable – but only to the extent they are recovered from the other party.

2. A 'Shared Risk' arrangement. In the event of losing, the Client pays a reduced fee to the Lawyer. If the case is won, fees are payable – but again, only to the extent they are recovered from the other party. The Solicitor

will require a 'success fee' (i.e. a mark-up because of the risk of losing the case and therefore earning nothing. The success fee comes out of the Client's damages award).

An After-the-Event (ATE) insurance policy is sometimes taken out to cover the opponent's costs if the case is lost. Normally, it is not possible to recover the costs of the ATE policy from the other side if you win the case. If there is no ATE insurance to cover the risk of paying the other party's costs, the Client may be faced with a very large bill if the case is lost.

Setting up a Conditional Fee Arrangement

If the Conditional fee arrangement does not meet the requirements, then it will be invalid and of no use. A key requirement is that the existence of such an arrangement is made known to all parties to the action (as soon as it is in place).

I will not go into lengthy detail about the CONDITIONAL and CONTINGENCY fee arrangements and the practical implications these have. However, I mention these to enable you to bring them up with your Solicitor if you feel the need to do so. However, if your Solicitor is going to do a proper job for you, they should advise you about these options anyway.

In the over-riding majority of cases, it is the 'after-the-event' insurance which is the important factor to assist in your decision making process on the costs and risks of your action (whether you are taking it against another party or you are defending yourself from another party).

Observations & Tips

- Insist that your Solicitor explores 'After-the-Event' (ATE) insurance for you (they should do this as a matter of course).

- Don't accept the explanation from your Solicitor that they have covered the insurance aspect by simply mentioning it in the small print of their Terms and Conditions.

- If an ATE insurance company will not take the risk on your case, then why should you?

- Please be aware that ATE insurance will only cover your legal costs in the event that your case is unsuccessful (i.e. it will not usually cover any separate award of damages against you).

- Do not forget to check your household or business insurance policy in case you have legal expenses cover. Do this as soon as possible because there may be a time-limit on making a claim.

CHAPTER 7

Dealing with Barristers and Q.C.s (or K.C.s)

Your Solicitor is the person responsible for liaising with Barristers and Q.C.s. Barristers and Q.C.s are commonly referred to as your 'Counsel'. In terms of day to day conduct of your case, you will have little contact with your Counsel's chambers.

What is a Barrister?

A Barrister is a practitioner of law who has been admitted to 'the Bar' and is permitted to appear in Court to argue a Client's case. Today, 'the Bar' is the commonly used name to describe a section of the legal profession.

The word 'bar' is a historical phrase - it comes from the short wall (or divide) in Court rooms which separates the Judges from the body of the Court. A Q.C. addresses the Judge from within the Bar. A Junior Barrister addresses the Judge at the Bar (or outside the Bar). A 'call to the bar' is a legal term of effect to describe how an individual has progressed to becoming a Barrister. A Barrister gets 'called to the bar' by one of the four Inns of Court (i.e. **Middle Temple, Inner Temple, Gray's Inn** or **Lincoln's Inn**).

In order to become a Barrister they must have attained the requisite honours degree and have attended a school of law to complete a valid course for a specific time period. They are required to pass the 'Bar final' exams before they can be called. The call is followed by a one year training at a Barrister's chambers where he or she works with a more experienced Barrister to learn the ropes which eventually leads them into the area of speciality they practice.

What is a Q.C. (or K.C.)?

Q.C. means 'Queen's Counsel'. The term applies to practitioners of the law who have been appointed to be 'Her Majesty's Counsel learned in the law'. A Q.C.

holds a higher legal rank than a Barrister. In order to qualify to be a Q.C. they usually have to serve as a Barrister (or as an 'advocate' in Scotland) for at least 10 years.

The term 'Queen's Counsel' can also be 'King's Counsel', depending on the reign of the Monarch.

Q.C.s are sometimes referred to as 'silks'. This stems from the fact that they wear silk gowns of a particular design whereas Junior Barristers gowns are called 'Stuff'. You may sometimes hear the phrase 'taking silk' to describe how a Barrister has become a Q.C.

[In Scotland, the Barrister equivalent is called an 'advocate'. Advocates are members of the Scottish Bar. They have the right to appear in all Scottish Courts. Queen's Counsel are called 'senior advocates'].

What is a Junior Barrister?

A Junior Barrister is a Barrister who has not attained the rank of Queen's Counsel (Q.C.). However, don't be fooled by the use of the description 'Junior' as indicative of a Barrister's inexperience. It is quite common for some junior Barristers to become very senior and to have practised for longer than some Q.C.s. Some Barristers practice for many years and deliberately do not 'take silk'. Junior Barristers who have been called to 'the bar' for over 10 years are sometimes referred to as 'Senior Juniors'.

The role of your Solicitor with your Counsel

Your Solicitor will instruct a Barrister or a Q.C. on your behalf after discussion with you on their suitability for your case. The Solicitor's firm is responsible for paying Counsel's fees but you will be billed for these by the Solicitor.

Your Barrister (or Q.C.) is the individual responsible for making your case in Court and developing the legal arguments to support your case. If you are the party taking the action (the Claimant), they will probably be involved in drafting a 'Pre–Action Protocol' letter to your opponent's Solicitors (i.e. like a notice advising them of pending legal action, setting out the reasons why a potential action is coming). Your Solicitor will send this letter to your opponent's Solicitors. Your Counsel will also prepare your claim (or defence) and be responsible for writing the detailed document which is eventually lodged in Court (the document is called a 'Particulars of Claim). Employing a Q.C. instead of a Junior Barrister is supposed to add a professional legal edge to your case (i.e. the advice you receive from Counsel is supposed to give a sort of 'gold standard' to bolster your case and how it is interpreted in law).

Having said that though, *you* have a key role to play in the way your Counsel prepares for the case. Invariably, you will meet your Barrister or Q.C. (sometimes more than once) in the lead up to your case.

Some Solicitors prefer Clients to say very little to Counsel and let the Barrister or Q.C. do the talking or the asking of questions.

Some Solicitors put Barristers and Q.C.s on a pedestal as if they are super-human legal Gods. However, in my experience, Barristers and Q.C.s are just human beings and they will appreciate any input from you (including you asking them questions). They are also capable of missing things and making mistakes just like any other member of the human race. It is therefore essential that you speak up at any meeting with them and leave no stone unturned about the issues which you feel are relevant to your case.

The ideal objective is to establish a partnership between Counsel, Solicitor and Client.

Counsel and your Witness Statement

Your Counsel will be employed to prepare a skeleton argument of your case which contains a summary of the facts, the relevant laws and an argument of how the law applies to the facts of your case. Counsel will probably also have a hand in writing your witness statement, along with input from your Solicitor. A word of warning I have for you is to firmly establish what strategy will be employed for arguing your case in Court before signing it.

What can happen is that you are given your witness statement (which has been written by your Solicitor and Counsel) and you get asked to sign it. You sign it because you think that your Counsel and Solicitor know what they are doing and know what needs to be said, even though you may want to add more to it or change it in some way. A tactic which I have seen employed by one Solicitor is to write a fairly short statement lacking in great detail because they don't want to give their tactical game away before trial on some of the main cross-examination points reserved for your opponent or their witnesses in Court.

By writing a short statement, your Counsel may want to raise or introduce the key issues by reference to documents or evidence at the trial itself. That is all very well. However, if you end up being asked to sign a short statement and your Counsel fails to stick to the game plan (i.e. forgets to ask the crucial questions or refer the Judge to critical evidence or documents), your case could be undermined and your credibility may be unnecessarily damaged in the eyes of the Judge. I am not kidding, there is every likelihood that if this happens and you complain to your Solicitor afterwards, you will probably be told that it's your fault for signing the statement which they wrote!

In my opinion, unless there is a very strong case for doing otherwise, or you have absolute faith in your Counsel to ask all the necessary questions and bring the relevant points to the Judge at trial, always write a detailed statement with cross references to documents and evidence – because that is what most Judges will rely on. It's a rarity to find yourself in a situation where you leave Court or the witness box and your Counsel has covered each and every point required. That's why I believe it is a good idea to have covered the points you want to make in your statement.

Meeting Counsel

When meeting with your Counsel it is very easy to get 'lulled' into a false sense of security because you feel there is someone expertly versed in the law on your side telling you that you have a good case 'in law', based on their interpretation of other legal cases similar to yours. You will probably think: "right, if that's what the law says then I must have a good case". You might think it is necessary to carry on regardless.

Stop right there.

Remove such thoughts from your mind.

Your Counsel should tell you that the law is never straightforward and therefore unpredictable. Hopefully, your case will be a good one – but I must stress that your opponent will have their own Counsel giving them a different interpretation of the law based on other legal cases to counter your position. So it is always advisable to retain a sense of caution, even if your case seems to be a strong one.

After my father's experience with litigation, I've come to the conclusion that litigation is really all about two sets of Barristers (or Q.C.s) getting the opportunity to put forward their respective legal arguments in Court – all at your expense. It's like a pantomime where they get the chance to have a sort of 'intellectual legal battle' between each other with no control over the outcome. Get the wrong Judge on the wrong day and you will lose the case. Get the right Judge on the right day and you will win. It's just a legal game. A gamble.

Don't look at it as if you are privileged to be using your Counsel's legal brains and expertise.

Look at it as if your Counsel is the privileged one because they are having the opportunity to put their legal arguments and thoughts in front of a Judge at your expense.

Certainly, treat them with the utmost respect because they can win your case if they do a good job. However, at the end of the day you are the customer and without you they wouldn't have the chance to put their legal ideas and thoughts into practice.

How can you tell if your Barrister has done a good job for you in Court?

Well, the answer to that is you can't until the Judgment is received. However, you should be able to get a good feel for how your Barrister has performed by assessing how matters unfolded in the Courtroom. Put the Court's procedural workings aside which the Barrister has to comply with and concentrate your assessment by imagining yourself in the Barrister's shoes.

Ask yourself this:

Did your Barrister cross-examine the witnesses fully, put all the arguments before the Judge and bring to the Court's attention all the evidence you wanted them to?

Did they do it in the manner you would have done if you had been the Barrister yourself?

If they did then it's probably fair to say that they did an acceptable job.

If the answer is no, then you should take it up with your Solicitor immediately and register your concerns. Put your concerns in writing as soon as possible after the hearing so they are on record before the Judgment arrives. Do not let yourself be talked out of making any complaint if your Solicitor tries to defend the performance of the Barrister.

My advice is always follow your 'gut instinct' because you will probably know the case better than anyone else. You are also probably the one paying – so it is essential that your concerns are registered. It will then be possible to evaluate your concerns against the Judgment when it finally arrives.

Observations & Tips

- Ask what cases your Counsel has been involved in before and what the results were (in their last 10 cases).

- Ask your Solicitor to provide copies of the Judgments in the cases which Counsel claims to have been involved. Take time to read these and see what the case (or cases) was (or were) about. What was the outcome? Do they seem to be the right Counsel for your case?

- When selecting a Barrister or Q.C. it is absolutely essential that the right one is employed for your case. For example, if you have a case which concerns professional negligence in a particular industry then your Solicitor should find a Barrister or Q.C. specialising in that field of litigation. It is their expert knowledge of the law in that area which can make the difference between winning or losing your case. Don't just accept your Solicitor's word that a Barrister or Q.C. will be suitable because they have worked with Counsel before on other unrelated cases to your own. Counsel must be highly experienced in the particular field of law you need them to be. Clients are guided by Solicitors when choosing Counsel and, in my opinion, it is not good enough for the Solicitor to just recommend a Barrister or Q.C. who is a 'jack of all trades' but 'master of none'.

- Don't hesitate to spell out to your Counsel what you feel your case is about if you get the chance to meet them.

- Listen to your Counsel with respect but don't be afraid to speak up if you don't agree or they have got something wrong. For example, if you want them to ask certain questions of your opponent in Court, put those questions in writing via your Solicitor. If they choose not to use them, then that's up to them – but if the case goes wrong because they failed to do as you asked, you have grounds for complaining.

- Remember, they are human beings and should be pleased to receive all your comments to assist them to get a better handle on your case.

- Just because your Counsel may say you have a strong case, don't forget that is just *one* opinion. Your opponent will no doubt be told that they have a good case too.

92

- Be wary of when a Q.C. says they want to work with a Junior Barrister to save money. The premise is to allow the Junior Barrister to do the ground work preparation on your case and the Q.C. puts it together at the end. However, in reality, use of both a Q.C. and a Junior Barrister can sometimes increase the cost unnecessarily (i.e. because you end up paying for two sets of fees and the Q.C. can sometimes spend a great deal of time dealing with it anyway). You should ask for an explanation on how the use of the two will actually save you money!

- Be careful when signing your witness statement. Make sure you are happy with it and it covers all the points you feel are critical. Remember, that's what the Judge should read.

- Check the contents and accuracy of the POC when it comes from the Q.C. or Barrister. Is it correct? Counsel sometimes prefer to stick to narrow legal arguments but in Court at the trial itself, Judges may want to know more background. Therefore, is there anything in the POC (or your Defence) which you think needs expanding? Remember, you will probably be asked to sign the statement of truth so you must be happy in yourself with it. The same can be said for your witness statement.

- Don't ever joke with Counsel – some take what you say literally, even if you are not being serious! Just be factual and businesslike. Otherwise, they may make a note or a reference to something at a later date (i.e. when they are writing the opinion for after the event insurance purposes) which is not actually true.

- Insist that you are sent written notes of all meetings with Counsel. Check whether they are accurate (i.e. do they contain all the key points which you recall). Remember, a note is only as good and accurate as the person making it. Sometimes things get missed. Therefore, it is also good practice to make your own notes of your meetings with Counsel.

- Sometimes Counsel can be so tied up in trying to think of complex legal arguments and issues on your case that they can miss the simple things. Therefore, never hesitate to make any point you think is necessary or say if you think they have missed anything. Remember, they are only human.

- *Never* praise Counsel or compliment them during your case. Only do that after you have won the case. They are paid to do a good job for you. Again, for the same reasons as not praising your Solicitor, they may otherwise claim that you were happy with them when you find yourself having to bring a negligence case against them or make a complaint.

- *Never* assume that a Judge in Court will look at all the bundles of evidence. Your Counsel must therefore bring all the relevant documents to his or her attention during the trial.

- Most Barristers and Q.C.'s have their own biographies/CV's on websites describing which cases they have been involved in. These appear on the websites of their Chambers. Curiously, these biographies/CV's rarely seem to say whether they won or lost those cases! Therefore, take time to look up the biography of your own Counsel and then ask them whether they were successful in those cases. You can do this when you meet them or do it through your Solicitor who can ask their clerk.

- During the trial you must keep a notepad handy and use it to pass messages/comments to your Barrister or Q.C. via your Solicitor. Your Solicitor will usually sit behind your Counsel and you will sit nearby. This message passing is to ensure that your Barrister or Q.C. do not overlook any points or arguments you wish them to make to the Judge. Remember, your Counsel is only human and can sometimes forget things as the matter unfolds in Court.

- If you find yourself in a situation where you are without the services of a Solicitor and you need legal assistance from a Barrister, but cannot afford to pay for it, you can get in touch with the 'Bar Pro Bono Unit' at the Bar Council. This is a charitable operation which helps to find free legal assistance from volunteer Barristers. Assistance from the 'Bar Pro Bono Unit' is available (in principle) to those who cannot afford to pay legal fees and cannot obtain public funding (Legal Aid). Assistance is not guaranteed for everyone but you will need to apply to the Unit either through a Solicitor or Advice Agency (i.e. Citizen's Advice Bureau or Law Centre). Further details can be found at ***www.barprobono.org.uk*** or at 'Bar Pro Bono Unit', The National Pro Bono Centre, 48 Chancery Lane, London WC2A IJF. Telephone 0207 092 3960. **PLEASE BEAR IN MIND THE UNIT IS A CHARITABLE ORGANISATION AND HAS LIMITED RESOURCES. THE WORK WHICH THE UNIT CARRIES OUT IS INVALUABLE TO THE PEOPLE IT HELPS. THE UNIT IS GRATEFUL FOR CHARITABLE DONATIONS.**

CHAPTER 8

Your Rights to Challenge your Bills

In an ideal world, everything would run smoothly, people would do exactly what they say they'll do and we'd all have nothing to be concerned about. In the real world, that doesn't always happen, especially where litigation is concerned.

Even with the implementation of the 'Costs Budgeting' regime imposed upon Lawyers, disputes can still arise over costs (even though the chances of this are supposedly reduced by the pre-agreed 'Costs Budget' in the earlier stages of the case).

If you receive a bill from your Solicitor which is excessive (or you are unhappy with matters relating to it or the service you have received from the firm), you must query it immediately. You have rights which allow you to have the bills checked – which I will come on to later.

Beware of the Time Limit

I have dedicated a chapter on the subject of getting your bills checked because there are strict time limits on when you can seek a formal assessment of these. If you want to ask a Court to assess them, you only get 12 months from the date the bill was paid (or sent).

As soon as the 12 months have passed you cannot normally ask a Court to assess the bill – even if there is a good reason for you not being able to within the 12 month limit.

So, even if you pay a bill in good faith but later discover that you have been over-charged (or there's an error), there is nothing you can do about it via the Court process after 12 months. In my opinion, the legislation effectively legalises fraud for Solicitors who have failed to act properly. So be warned!

You may think that it won't be an issue (because 12 months may seem a long enough time). However, in reality, that is not necessarily true.

A practical difficulty exists for all Clients when Solicitors submit their bills because you will generally pay the bills 'as you go'. It is rare for a Solicitor to wait until the end of your case and send you the whole bill 'in one go'. You can find that your case goes on for over a year – or even several years. Therefore, you may have paid bills in the early stages in good faith but by the time your case reaches Court (or ends) the bills paid can be out of time. In fact, this was one of the issues which came up in my father's case when we discovered how much my father had been over-charged. We never knew about the 12 month time limit and nothing could be done about it via the Court route. Despite our complaints to the firm of Solicitors at the time concerning the overcharging, they just hid behind the time limit rule and refused to answer them.

Another problem you may face is what to do if you discover over-charging or poor service by your Solicitor mid-way through your case. For example, you may be near the trial and you are being told that you should win, yet you discover an over-charge or you have an issue over service.

Do you let it go because you don't want to cause a fuss when you may win the case anyway?

Do you bite your tongue for fear of the Solicitor stopping work (they call it 'going off the record') and you having to issue proceedings against them when they should otherwise be getting on with your case?

It can be a real dilemma. From experience, you should always raise any issue immediately and don't keep quiet. However, I will tell you how you might get around the problem later in this chapter.

There are various ways in which you can have your bills checked, either through a Court or via the Legal Ombudsman in England and Wales or The Law Society's Complaints Department in Scotland or Northern Ireland. Remember too that the Legal Ombudsman and The Law Societies have different powers than a Court in the assessment of bills. In fact, The Law Society has the power to reduce a Solicitor's bill even after it has been reduced by a Judge in Court. The case of *Regina v The Council of The Law Society ex parte Pictons Smeathmans [CO/1197/95]* upholds this, where Mr Justice Tuckey stated in paragraphs B & C on page 8 of his Judgment on The Law Society's powers:

"...... One sees no such limitation in those provisions. The right to determine costs should be limited is not confined in that way. Paragraph 2 (2) makes it clear that it may relate to money which the client has already paid, or someone else has already paid on his behalf, to the solicitor. So the power to make a determination is unlimited."

Therefore, the Legal Ombudsman or The Law Societies have the power to reduce a Solicitor's bill to zero, in theory, if it decides such a reduction is warranted. I will discuss that option after I have set out the other options for getting your bills assessed.

If a Solicitor fails to give you a proper explanation as to why their costs are so much more than the estimate provided to you, then ask the Solicitor to look up Paragraph 26 in the Judgment of a case called *Leigh v Michelin Tyre PLC [2003] EWCA Civ 1766.* This is a case which went to the Court of Appeal in which Lord Justice Dyson stated:

"..... the estimates made by solicitors of the overall likely costs of the litigation should usually provide a useful yardstick by which the reasonableness of the costs finally claimed may be measured. If there is a substantial difference between the estimated costs and the costs claimed, that difference calls for an explanation. In the absence of a satisfactory explanation, the court may conclude that the difference itself is evidence from which it can conclude that the costs claimed are unreasonable."

You may also want to keep another case law in mind of *Reynolds v Stone Rowe Brewer (2008) EWHC 497 (QB).* Again, this case upholds the principle that a Solicitor should only be paid what is reasonable and cannot expect to be paid more than an original estimate, unless the Solicitor can justify the extra costs with good reason.

A distinction exists between a 'paid' bill and an 'unpaid' bill. If the bill is unpaid, a Client can ask the Court to order an assessment of the bill if he or she can demonstrate special circumstances, even if it was sent to them more than 12 months before the application to have the assessment was made.

What is the normal process for getting bills assessed?

Normally, you should receive your bill within a reasonable time after your Solicitor has finished their work for you. The bill should be made up of 3 elements:

1. Disbursements (i.e. like Counsel's fees)

2. VAT

3. Solicitor's fees

All bills must be signed by a partner of the firm. If they are not then the bill is invalid.

If your fees relate to 'Court work', the fees your Solicitor charges are subject to Court rules. If your fees relate to 'non Court work', then there are no precise scales which regulate it but the charges your Solicitor makes must be fair and reasonable.

If you feel that your bill is too high you can either:

1. Ask your Solicitor for a detailed account (an itemised bill) so that you can study it and compare it with the estimate you were given.

2. Complain to the Legal Ombudsman (or relevant Law Society) and ask them to investigate the matter.

3. Ask a Court to look at your bill (commonly known as 'Cost Assessment').

1.   Getting a detailed bill from your Solicitor

Write to your Solicitor to ask for the detailed bill. You should ask for their response to be sent to you in writing.

Once you receive the detailed bill, study it closely in comparison to the estimates you were given. Check the written summaries (narratives) on the bill to see what your Solicitor has claimed to have done in return for the fees charged. Does it make sense? Is the bill signed by a partner? Does the hourly rate charged reflect what you were told it was going to be? Is it way out from the estimates given?

2.   Complain to the Legal Ombudsman (or relevant Law Society)

If you are not happy with the bill then you can complain to the Legal Ombudsman or relevant Law Society. They will investigate your concerns and reduce your Solicitor's bill if they agree with your complaint. There is no charge for this service. See Chapter 10 for details.

3.   Asking a Court to examine the bill

This procedure can be used for any work done by a Solicitor, including 'Court work'. It is known as 'Assessment' or sometimes 'Taxation'.

The Court can examine the whole bill and can either approve it or reduce it. You should be advised that if the Court reduces the bill by more than 20% then you will not be required to pay for the assessment process and the costs will have to be met by your Solicitor. Otherwise, you would be required to pay the costs of the process.

If you ask for an assessment within 1 month of receiving the bill, the Court must assess it. Between 1 month and 12 months the Court will decide whether to agree to assess the bill. After a year, it is very unusual for the Courts to agree to assessing the bill. Again, the Court cannot assess the bill if it has been paid and more than 1 year has gone by.

If you have a problem paying the bill

If you are having problems in paying a Solicitor's bill, your Solicitor might try to get an immediate payment (and they could also charge you interest for 'non Court work' after a month). They may agree to allow you to pay your bill by instalments. Some Solicitors might even suggest taking a 'charge' on your property (i.e. like securing the debt against your house, car or the like). However, I would strongly advise against such a measure unless you are totally happy with it and you have received proper legal advice on the implications. If you miss payments they can take enforcement proceedings and make you sell up in order to get their payment. To be quite frank, if a Solicitor ever finds themselves in a situation where the idea of a charge is put forward, they haven't done their job properly. Somewhere along the line there must have been a failure to assess your situation or advise on costs.

A Costs Draftsman

A Costs Draftsman is somebody who can assess and scrutinise your costs. He or she is technically known as a 'Law Costs Draftsman'.

A Costs Draftsman can work for a specialist cost assessment firm or work for themselves as a self-employed specialists. You can even find a Costs Draftsman employed in a permanent in-house position at a firm of Solicitors (usually the larger firms). You can employ a Costs Draftsman to assist you to resolve your dispute on a bill.

A good Costs Draftsman will properly assess your bills. Find a good one and he or she can be worth their weight in gold. Costs draftsmen are concerned with all aspects of Solicitor's costs. In general, they get involved in the following areas:

1. Solicitor's costs payable by a Client

Costs payable by you to your Solicitor. If you are unhappy with your bill you can challenge it and either party (Solicitor or you) can apply to the Court for the bill to be assessed. A Costs Draftsman can be employed to prepare a formal bill of cost to be lodged with the Court as well as advising on the procedures. He or she can also argue in support or oppose the bill.

2. Costs payable between you and your opponent

If you lose your case you will usually be ordered to pay the winner's costs (as long as they are reasonable – however, you will rarely have to pay these in full).

If the costs cannot be agreed by negotiation between you and your opponent then a formal bill will be produced. The paying party will serve what are called 'Points of Dispute'. These are the points of disagreement on the costs charged. The receiving party has the opportunity to serve a reply to the 'Points of Dispute' before the bill is lodged with a Court.

A Court hearing then takes place where points of issue are considered by a 'Costs Judge'. The Costs Judge makes a decision on what is fair and reasonable. A Costs Draftsman is often instructed to prepare the formal bill as well as draft the replies to the points of dispute. You can have a Costs Draftsman representing one party and another Costs Draftsman representing the other party. They can both attend the costs hearing in the Court.

3. Legal Aid costs

In situations where a Solicitor is representing you as a Legal Aid Client, a Costs Draftsman may be employed to make submissions. A formal bill of costs is normally required so that the costs can be assessed by the Court. Normally, these bills are assessed without a formal hearing but if a Solicitor wishes to challenge, a hearing can be arranged.

What is the best way to challenge bills?

I can't tell you the best way to challenge your bill because it will depend on your circumstances and how you found yourself in the situation. However, The Law Society/Legal Ombudsman route can be a sensible way to do it. Not only is it a free service but The Law Society and Legal Ombudsman have different powers over a Solicitor than a Court.

Irrespective of what happens in a 'costs assessment' in Court, you can still refer the matter to the Legal Ombudsman or Law Society, especially if you believe you have received inadequate professional service from your Solicitor. However, you should advise the relevant Complaints Organisation that you wish to make a complaint (before the Court assessment process begins) so they have it on record and you avoid the time limit restrictions which might otherwise apply.

How to avoid the time limit restrictions

In order to avoid the time limit restrictions when challenging your bill you must seek to arrange matters with your Solicitor at the outset of your case, so that no time limits apply to you.

You can do this by asking your Solicitor to agree to waiving any time limit restrictions when you sign your Terms of Engagement (or getting your Solicitor to extend the time period to beyond the 12 months). You must make it a condition of your own Terms of Engagement with your Solicitor (this is one of the areas which will be covered in the 'Terms of Engagement' in Chapter 11).

If your case has already begun, you can request that your Solicitor does not impose any time restrictions if you have cause to query a bill. A professional and reasonable Solicitor should have no objections to that request. If they do object then you might ask yourself why. Is it because they have got something to worry about? If they have done a proper job for you then the Solicitor should have no problem agreeing to your request. At the end of the day, all you are asking them to do is consenting to have any disputed costs assessed by a Costs Judge and for the Solicitor to stand by the findings of that Judge. Is that really so unreasonable?

Observations & Tips

- You might find that some Solicitors will refuse to waive the time limit on having their bills assessed, seeking to rely on the fact that there is no legal requirement for them to do so (and you might be told that a Court does not have the jurisdiction to refer bills to an assessment of the relevant time period has expired). How you feel about that and how you deal with that matter is up to you - but if the Solicitor refuses to waive the time limit, at least you will be aware of the importance of checking and querying every bill you receive when it arrives. You must raise any concerns about any bill you receive and ask for a written explanation.

- Raise any concerns about a bill at the earliest opportunity.

- Remember, check if your bill has been signed by a partner of the firm. If not, the bill is invalid.

- If you discover after a costs assessment in Court that you've been over-charged by more than 50%, all the partners of the firm get reported to their Regulator and are subject to disciplinary action for the offence of 'culpable overcharging'. If you suspect this may be the case, it is worth reminding your Solicitor of that fact. They might seek a compromise deal with you.

- If you get a huge bill that you were not expecting then immediately query it with your Solicitor. Have they spent hours going around in circles because they did not know what they were doing? Have they used other fee earners at the firm to do work without telling you?

- Ask to see the Solicitor's **time-sheets** so that you can analyse the bill. Don't just rely on the narratives which accompany your bills. Scrutinise the time-sheets and compare them to the work actually done.

- Be wary if your Solicitor says they want to involve a team of fee earners to work on your case. They may quote an hourly rate to you for themselves but if they involve another two or three people, the rate will rocket. Is a team of people necessary when your Solicitor should be doing the job themselves? How much time are they going to spend reading up the case, discussing it or duplicating tasks which have already been done? You must question the sense in having such a team.

- Be aware that you will be charged for things like accommodation (if your Solicitor has to make a trip to see a witness and stay overnight). Check where they stay because there is no justification for them staying in a 5 Star hotel when alternative accommodation is available. Why should they stay in a luxury hotel at your expense?

- If you require the services of a Cost Draftsman then you should approach **The Association of Law Costs Draftsmen** at *www.alcd.org.uk*.

CHAPTER 9

The Different Approaches taken by a Court

when Assessing Costs

A comment you may hear during the course of your dealings with your Solicitor is that the costs being incurred (both your own and your opponent's) will be checked on 'Assessment' or 'Taxation' at the end of your case.

In other words, you may be left with the impression that there's an official 'standard' process which will ensure that all the costs are fair. You may also be under the impression that this process is short and simple. However, in my experience, I can tell you that the assessment process is not simple or quick at all. Depending on your case, the assessment process can take months and be a costly exercise in its own right. Not only this, but if you've won your case, you may be left waiting for your costs for a considerable period of time and find that the costs you eventually receive back are much less than you were expecting.

What I'm saying here is that the assessment process should also be explained to you at the beginning of your case because it is another crucial factor in the painting of the whole picture of your case. You need to know about it because you need to consider it when making your decision about whether to proceed with your action or not. In my experience, Solicitors generally seem to refer to the assessment process as a throw-away remark. However, you should be advised that the outcome of the assessment process can go in any number of different directions for you (good and bad) and it is not straightforward by any means.

With the introduction of the 'Costs Budgeting' process, this should make the assessment of your bills more straightforward (i.e. because the costs will have effectively been pre-agreed and sanctioned by the Court - thus making it difficult to deviate from them). However, the 'Costs Budgeting' principles do not apply to all situations and do not apply to cost assessments on what is called the

'Indemnity' basis. The principle of 'Costs Budgeting' is really only applicable for costs assessed on the 'Standard' basis.

Don't worry! I will explain what is meant by 'Indemnity' and 'Standard' later in this Chapter.

So, why it is not straightforward?

As you know, more often than not, the winning party in litigation will only be able to recover part of their Solicitor's fees and any other expenses which have been incurred to progress the case to a conclusion.

Even if you win, payment of the fees is your own personal responsibility (as you are the one who made a contract with your Solicitor to pay them). That includes disbursements (i.e. Barrister's fees, expert's fees and Court fees).

Your Solicitor must ensure that the amount of fees charged is reasonable and equates with the extent and quality of the work done and the legal advice provided.

"That's all very well", you may say, *"But if I win the fees owed to my Solicitor will be paid by my opponent at the end of the day"*.

Well, *not* necessarily!

A common misconception by most lay-people involved in litigation is that getting their costs back after victory in Court is a foregone conclusion. I'm sorry to have to tell you but there are different ways in which the legal system treats your costs and differences in rights you have to see your outlay replenished – and these are not straightforward.

There are 2 bases of cost assessment. These are the (1) **Standard basis** or the (2) **Indemnity basis.**

(1) Standard basis

On the 'Standard basis' the winning party is entitled to recover costs which have been reasonably incurred and those costs are reasonable in amount (provided that the total of costs is reasonably proportionate to the issues of the case).

(2) Indemnity basis

On the 'Indemnity basis' the burden of proof showing the costs are reasonable is shifted compared to the 'Standard basis'. The loser pays all of the winner's costs (except those costs which are shown to have been unreasonably incurred or are unreasonable in amount paid).

There is also no question of proportionality being applied on the 'Indemnity basis'.

So, on average, even on the 'Indemnity basis', the level of recovery from the losing party is not likely to be more than 80% of the costs.

The **Indemnity** principle is really concerned with the relationship between the winning party and their own Lawyers. The costs which a party may recover from the other are those costs which the winning party is liable to pay. The losing party's liability is to 'indemnify' (secure) the winning party against the winner's liability for costs.

The losing party does not become directly responsible to pay the winning party's Solicitor's fees directly to the Solicitor concerned – the responsibility for payment of those fees remains with the Client (whether or not the losing party actually has the money to pay them – so you could find yourself financially 'screwed' if you win and the other party cannot pay. Your own Solicitor will pursue *you* for payment of their fees). The losing party cannot be sued by the winning party's Solicitor for non-payment of those fees because there is no contract between them and the losing party.

The Right to Challenge

Any person faced with the direct payment of their own Solicitor's fees (or indirect payment by indemnity of their opponent's Solicitor's fees) has the right to ask a Court to assess whether or not the sums of money claimed are fair and reasonable.

If such a request is made by the losing party, the Costs Judge will apply either the **Standard basis** or the **Indemnity basis** for assessment purposes, depending on the situation.

This is a fundamental point of which you need to be aware.

What basis will be applied in which circumstance?

If a Client wishes to *challenge the amount of their own Solicitor's fees*, the '**Indemnity basis**' will be applied by the Court.

If the losing party wishes *to challenge a claim made against them by the winning party to recover the winning party's Solicitor's fees,* a different basis called the '**Standard basis**' will be applied by the Court.

In order to understand why the losing party would usually only have to fund part of the winning party's Solicitor's fees, it is important to appreciate the difference between the 2 bases of approach adopted by the legal system.

I will explain the difference between the 2 bases but the fundamental point is that the system differentiates between the *paying* party and the *receiving* party – i.e. who has to discharge the burden of proof and show if the costs charged are fair and reasonable?

On assessment of costs on a '**Standard basis**' (i.e. the loser pays the winner), the Court will only allow costs which correspond in amount to the matters of issue and will resolve any doubt in favour of the paying party (i.e. the loser). The Court will take into account the sums of money involved, the importance of the case, the complexity of the issues and the financial position of each party and all circumstances in general.

Obviously, by the time a Costs Judge is asked to carry out a detailed assessment of the costs of the winning party, the costs will already have been incurred (so any arguments about the fairness and proportionality should be quite limited because of the original 'Costs Budget' agreed when the claim was lodged in Court).

On assessment of costs on an **'Indemnity basis'** (i.e. Client pays their own Solicitor), proportionality does *not* apply – although the Court will still not allow costs which have been unreasonably incurred or are unreasonable in amount. Any doubt on this basis will generally be given to the receiving party (i.e. the Solicitor).

Please note:

A Court will normally order that the losing party pay the winning party's costs on the **Standard** basis. However, the Court can sometimes order these costs are paid on the **Indemnity** basis if the losing party's conduct justifies it.

In Summary

For the avoidance of doubt, the losing party in litigation does not become contractually responsible to pay the Solicitor's fees incurred by the winning party. The winning party is only entitled to claim the replenishment of their own Solicitor's fees from the losing party as if it was additional 'compensation'. More often then not, the winning party will only be awarded part of the fees (usually the majority) they have incurred with their own Solicitor – not the totality of those fees.

IMPORTANT NOTE
IF YOU HAVE YOUR COSTS ASSESSED IN COURT

You must show the Court how you relied on the cost estimate given to you

When a Solicitor provides a cost estimate to a Client, it follows that the Solicitor should be made to keep to that estimate. In fact, it should go without saying because it is as logical as night follows day. It should also go without saying that any Client would rely on that estimate because it is a material *'representation'* made by a Solicitor which:

(a)   Enables a Client to decide how to apply resources to the legal action (i.e. arrange finances by a loan, drawing from savings or seeking insurance).

(b)   Enables a Client to decide whether or not to proceed with the action (i.e. to weigh up the cost and risk).

(c)   Induces a Client to act accordingly (i.e. in both (a) and (b) above).

Well, let me tell you something which may shock you.

Whether you are having the *'Solicitor/Client'* bills assessed or the *'Loser/Winner'* bills assessed, some Costs Judges at Cost Assessments might not automatically expect the original cost estimate given by the Solicitor to be adhered to by the Solicitor concerned. Some Costs Judges might expect the Client to show how he or she relied on the estimate in the first place!

Yes, an illogical and perverse aspect of legal procedure (which, to be fair was something which occurred in the days prior to 'Costs Budgeting', rather than today).

I mean, what else does a Client have to rely upon other than the estimate provided by the Solicitor?

111

What is the purpose of the Solicitor providing the cost estimate if it is not to be relied upon?

Without an estimate, a Client has nothing to rely upon and therefore nothing to enable him or her to plan their finances or even decide whether to proceed with the action or not.

I am not joking. In the days before 'Costs Budgeting ', some Costs Judges at Assessment expected Clients to prove to the Court how they relied on the estimate provided by a Solicitor. For example, in theory, it was a therefore possible (prior to the introduction of 'Costs Budgeting') to see a Client given an estimate of £50,000 by a Solicitor and then see the Solicitor charge them £100,000. When the Client disputed the cost in Court some Costs Judges did not require the Solicitor to explain how their charges had exceeded the estimate. They expected the Client to prove how they relied on the original estimate. It seemed as if some of these Judges expected cost estimates to be exceeded by Solicitors as a matter of course and the Client was bound to pay more than he was told he would need to. A complete farce. In fact, such a stance flew in the face of the Solicitor's professional obligations under Law Society rules on cost information.

In any situation where reason and logic applies, the onus to show why a cost estimate should not be relied upon should be on the Solicitor. The onus should not be on the Client to prove that he relied on the estimate.

In my opinion, when a Solicitor has provided a cost estimate then the Solicitor should be held to that estimate. Pure and simple. The only situation where a Solicitor would not be held to the estimate would be:

1. If the Solicitor tells the Client that the estimate is not to be relied upon (which would be perverse in itself because there would be no point in the Solicitor supplying the estimate in the first place).

2. The Client terminates his or her retainer with the Solicitor.

3. The instructions from the Client deviate from the advice given by the Solicitor.

When none of the above applies, a Client should not have to provide evidence that he relied on the cost estimate given to him by the Solicitor. In my opinion, it should be an automatic presumption by the Judge that the Client relied on the estimate given to him. If the Costs Judge chooses to make an issue of 'reliance' at any Court Assessment, it should be for the charging Solicitor to prove that a Client could not have relied on the estimate.

This view is supported by a House of Lords authority which has stood for over 130 years. In the case of **Smith v Chadwick (1884) 9 App Cas 187**, Lord Blackburn at paragraph 196 said:

> "I think that if it is proved that the defendants with a view to induce the plaintiff to enter into a contract made a statement to the plaintiff of such a nature as would be likely to induce a person to enter into a contract, and it is proved that the plaintiff did enter into the contract, it is a fair inference of fact that he was induced to do so by the statement ..."

In what lay-person's terms, this means that if a Solicitor tells you that the cost is going to be 'X' and you then decide to proceed with the action based on this information, it is fair to assume that you relied on that information (and that you were induced to act by it).

Bizarrely, some Costs Judges seemed to ignore this legal authority and expected a Client to prove that he or she relied on an estimate when there is a dispute over the costs charged. Like I say, this was a more common occurrence in the days before the introduction of 'Costs Budgets' where the Court now has a greater control over the costs. The issue should (in theory) be redundant now because the costs should have been agreed beforehand.

Nevertheless, the critical point I am trying to make is that, in the context of proving 'reliance' on a cost estimate before a Costs Judge, it is imperative that you do not take any chances. If an estimate has been exceeded then you must make sure that your Cost Draftsman (or legal representative) shows the Judge how you relied on the estimate. Do not assume that the Judge will make a Solicitor keep to the estimate without such proof of reliance.

In order to make your case as strong as possible in Court, you should provide a statement (with documentary evidence, if possible) explaining how you relied on the estimate given to you by the Solicitor. For example, you may have taken out a loan with a bank or borrowed money from somebody. You may also have attempted to take out after-the-event insurance. These are valuable pieces of evidence which can show the Court how you relied on the estimate. For example, you could use the evidence of the loan agreement to show the Judge or use the evidence of the insurer's quotation for insurance to show how the estimate was relied upon to work out the insurance premium.

I am compelled to bring this to your attention because some Solicitors who act for Clients at Cost Assessments over disputed fees charged by another Solicitor, do not always take the time to explain to a Costs Judge how the Client relied on the estimate. They assume that, just because there is a difference between the estimate provided and the bill finally charged, the Judge will take the overcharging Solicitor to task. Of course, in the real world (where common sense prevails more than it does in the legal world), the Client should not have to show reliance because the Costs Judge should expect that the Client relied on the estimate provided. However, an unacquainted legal representative acting for a Client in a fee dispute at a Cost Assessment may simply not be aware of the risk that a Costs Judge may take a perverse approach over 'reliance'.

So, please make sure that your representations are made in full to the Costs Judge!

Observations & Tips

- Remember, the assessment process on costs can be drawn out and costly in itself. It's not all over when the Judgment is given.

- Ask your Solicitor to explain the assessment process to you when you meet them at the outset.

- If you have a dispute over the fees charged by a Solicitor, you must demonstrate to the Costs Judge how you relied on the estimate provided by that Solicitor.

CHAPTER 10

What If You Have a Complaint about a Solicitor?

If a Solicitor has managed your case and your expectations properly, you should have no reason to complain. However, if you are unhappy with any part of your Solicitor's work you must advise the firm as soon as possible and put your complaint in writing.

Do *not* linger in silence when you feel let down in the hope that it won't matter in the end. Do *not* leave your complaint until long after the case is ended.

You may have an issue over excessive charges, delay, failure to keep you advised or not being treated fairly or with respect. You may be unhappy because your Solicitor has just not met your expectations of what you consider to be an acceptable level of *service*. You may also be unhappy with the *conduct* of your Solicitor.

Under the 'Client Care' obligations, part of your Solicitor's duty is that the firm has to have a complaints procedure in place to deal with your concerns. You must therefore inform your Solicitor immediately or contact the Complaints Partner at the firm (the name of whom should have been advised to you in your original 'Client Care' letter). Therefore, your Solicitor has a professional obligation to deal with your complaint effectively.

Under professional regulations, Solicitors are required to handle your complaint in a fair and respectful manner.

A Solicitor should *not*:

- Be aggressive or defensive to you or suffer 'wounded pride'.
- Reject your complaint immediately without good reason.
- Give the impression that they know all the answers.
- Forget that you are the Client (and therefore their livelihood) and you have needs and expectations which the Solicitor should care about.

- Be critical if you have requested money as a remedy.
- Charge you for investigating your complaint/s.

A Solicitor can sometimes turn from your ally into your enemy when you make a complaint (and you end up having to fight against more than your original opponent in the legal action). If this happens, it can be a most distressing time because you may find yourself in a situation where your Solicitor decides to 'down tools' and stops working and then pulls out all the tricks from their bag to make your life as difficult as possible – just to protect their own interests. In situations like those, Solicitors who behave like that soon forget your own interests and your original case. However, part of any complaints investigation process is to review how a Solicitor actually handles your complaint.

So, don't be put off if you find that your Solicitor behaves unreasonably or aggressively to defend themselves. He or she will ultimately be answerable to their own Regulator.

In England and Wales, the Legal Ombudsman can only deal with matters of 'poor service' (please see Glossary at rear of this book). However, if your complaint is concerned with the 'conduct' of a Solicitor then it will need to be referred up to the Solicitors Regulation Authority (SRA). As mentioned before, the SRA is the independent regulatory arm of The Law Society (the top layer of The Law Society cake, so to speak). Complaints can often include both 'poor service' and bad 'conduct'. Therefore you should refer the matter first to the Legal Ombudsman or relevant Law Society. They should refer matters of 'conduct' up to the SRA.

In reality, there is actually no harm in contacting the SRA directly yourself if your complaint is only about 'conduct'. The SRA can currently be contacted on 0870 606 2555 or *www.sra.org.uk* (for England and Wales).

Poor service

So, what is poor service? Typical examples of poor service are as follows:

- Failure to provide written costs estimates (or on-going costs estimates).

- Errors in billing.

- Failure to properly explain the risks of the litigation.

- Failure to carry out a cost/risk/benefit analysis (and failure to keep a Client regularly updated on it).

- Failure to respond to communications (i.e. letters, phone calls, emails etc).

- Failure to act on an issue the Solicitor agreed to deal with.

- Not treating the Client with fairness or respect.

- Failing to have a complaints procedure.

- Lack of 'Client Care' information.

Additional issues which can be indicative of poor service are:

- Deceiving or misleading the Client.

- Terminating the retainer unreasonably.

- Not adhering to a quotation.

- Failure to provide written evidence of advice given.

- Failure to inform of progress.

- Failure to follow instructions.

Procedure for Complaining

Having advised the firm of your complaint(s), your concerns should be investigated by the Complaints Partner (or if you have sent them to the Solicitor, he or she should initially report back to you).

If you are still not happy after receiving a response you should contact The Law Society. As stated before, in England and Wales, The Law Society relies on the services of an independent organisation called the 'Legal Ombudsman' to investigate complaints about poor service against Solicitors. At the time of writing this book, the contact details for the different Law Societies are as follows:

England and Wales

The Law Society of England & Wales
The Law Society's Hall
113 Chancery Lane
London WC2A 1PL
Tel: +44 (0) 20 7242 1222
Fax: +44 (0) 20 7831 0344
www.lawsociety.org.uk

Scotland

The Law Society of Scotland
Atria One,
144 Morrison Street,
Edinburgh EH3 8EX
Tel: +44 (0) 131 226 7411
Fax: +44 (0) 131 225 2934
www.lawscot.org.uk

Northern Ireland

The Law Society of Northern Ireland
96 Victoria Street
Belfast   BT2 8BA

Tel: +44 (0) 28 90 231614
Fax: +44 (0) 28 90 232606
www.lawsoc-ni.org.uk

As far as procedure is concerned, you should first try to resolve your complaint with your Solicitor. All firms are required to have a written complaints procedure. The Solicitor must give you a copy of this if you request it.

If you are not satisfied you can contact the relevant Law Society and ask to be referred to the relevant complaints handling organisation. They can advise you on how to proceed and discuss your case in principle (i.e. tell you if you have grounds for a complaint). If the matter is concerned with a 'service' issue with a Solicitor then you will probably be referred to the Legal Ombudsman in England and Wales. However, the Ombudsman will first ask you to try and resolve the matter with the firm of Solicitors concerned.

A Solicitor has 8 weeks to resolve your complaint. If you are still not satisfied (or they fail to deal with your complaint after 8 weeks) then you can refer the matter to the Legal Ombudsman. You have 6 months to bring your complaint to the Ombudsman following a final response from a Solicitor. Please note that the Legal Ombudsman requires any complaint to be brought to the organisation no later than 12 months from when the problem first occurred (or from when you should reasonably have become aware of the problem). Therefore, you should not delay in bringing any complaint to the Ombudsman's attention.

Under the SRA Code of Conduct Rules on dealing with complaints, a Solicitor is required to inform you of your right to refer the matter to the Legal Ombudsman and give you the contact details for the Ombudsman. The Solicitor is also required to inform you of the time deadlines. If your Solicitor does not do so, they will have not complied with the SRA's complaints handling rules.

You will need to fill out a form which the Legal Ombudsman will send you on request. The Ombudsman will consider your complaint and, if appropriate, may order your Solicitor to:

1. Refund money which you have paid.

2. Correct any mistakes or take any other necessary action at their own expense.

3. Pay you compensation.

4. Apologise to you.

5. Give back any documents you might need.

If your Solicitor is found to have broken any of the rules of conduct, they may be referred to the relevant disciplinary body.

Fraud, Dishonesty and Misconduct

If you believe that a Solicitor is committing fraud (i.e. making false representations to gain material advantage) or is just dishonest, this is a matter for the SRA to deal with. The SRA is alive to the fact that the greatest risks to the public and consumers of legal services are fraud, dishonesty and serious misconduct. The SRA has a special Fraud Department which investigates dishonesty and serious misconduct. Examples of the type of misconducts associated with fraud and dishonesty are as follows:

- Mis-use of funds from the Client Money Account.

- Suspected money laundering through the Profession.

- Mortgage fraud.

- Abandonment of the case or sudden closure of the firm.

- Arrest, charge or conviction.

- Suspected dishonesty.

- Financial problems.

- A person pretending to be Solicitor.

These are typical issues which the Fraud Department of the SRA deal with but the list is not supposed to be exhaustive. If you believe that a Solicitor is acting in a fraudulent manner or is dishonest or behaving in a manner which could fall under the description of misconduct, then you must report this to the SRA. The contact number for the SRA is 0370 606 2555 (General Enquiries). The confidential telephone number for the Fraud Department is 0345 850 0999 (you can also e-mail the Department confidentially at *redalert@sra.org.uk*).

For your information, the current contact details of the SRA are:

Solicitors Regulation Authority
The Cube
199 Wharfside Street
Birmingham
B1 1RN
Tel: 0370 606 2555 (General Enquiries). 0345 850 0999 (Fraud Investigation Department) or at *www.sra.org.uk*

Complaints about Barristers and Q.C.'s

If you have a complaint about a Barrister or Q.C. then you can refer the matter to 'The Bar Council'. This is the approved Regulator of the Bar of England and Wales which discharges its regulatory functions through the independent 'Bar Standards Board'. A complaint should normally go first to the Barrister's Chambers and then to the Bar Standards Board. At the time of writing, the contact details are as follows (where you can find out the procedure for complaining):

The Bar Council
289-293 High Holborn
London WC1V 7HZ
Tel: +44 (0) 20 7242 0082
Fax: +44 (0) 20 7831 9217
www.barcouncil.org.uk

Complaints about Judges

If you have a complaint about the conduct or behaviour of a Judge then you can refer the matter to the 'Judicial Conduct and Investigations Office' (JCIO). At the time of writing, the contact details are as follows:

Judicial Conduct Investigation Office (JCIO)
81-82 Queens Building
Royal Courts of Justice
Strand
London WC2A 2LL
Fax: +44 (0) 20 7073 4725
www.judicialconduct.judiciary.gov.uk

A Suggestion

Over the years the organisations investigating complaints about Solicitors have changed and been known by several different names. It can be quite confusing and difficult to know where to go. If you do have a complaint which has not been resolved by the firm, I would suggest that you contact the relevant professional body as soon as possible. The body will tell you which complaints handling organisation will deal with it.

Observations & Tips

- Do not ever feel awkward about making a complaint (whether it's about a Solicitor, Barrister, Q.C. or Judge). Take the time to set out your concerns and get them investigated.

- Do not delay in raising any complaints you have (and make sure you do not hold back when making them – be bold). If complaining about a Solicitor, make sure you do not fall outside the time deadline for making your complaint to The Law Society/Legal Ombudsman. If you are in any doubt, contact The Law Society at the earliest opportunity for guidance and get them to register your concerns.

- Raise the issues as soon as they arise and don't leave it until after your case has ended (otherwise it may look like a case of 'sour grapes' to third party – even though you know it isn't!).

- Keep a record of conversations, meetings and times in your diary and record what you were told. These will prove invaluable evidence in supporting any concerns you may have at a later date.

- If you reside in a country outside the UK and the legal system is founded on English law, please contact The Law Society or relevant regulatory body in that country via the internet or telephone directory service. You should be able to contact the relevant organisation that will help or deal with your complaint.

- **A tip for people who have carried out work for a Solicitor in a professional capacity and you have not been paid for some time**: If a Solicitor has used you to provide professional services to their firm and your bill has remained unpaid for an unreasonable length of time, you should politely (but firmly) point out to the Solicitor that failure to pay the debt owed to you is a breach of one of the compulsory Core Duties of a Solicitor. **SRA Core Duty 8** states that: *A Solicitor must run their* *business or carry out their role in the business effectively and in accordance with proper governance and sound financial and risk management principles.* If a firm is carrying a debt to you for an unpaid invoice, it could be argued that the firm has not met its obligations under proper governance and sound financial management principles. If the firm ignores your payment reminders then tell the firm that you will be contacting the SRA if you do not receive payment. The SRA telephone number is 0370 606 2555.

CHAPTER 11

Protecting Your Interests

<u>Issuing Your Own Terms of Engagement</u>

I hope you will have found this book helpful in highlighting important points which you should be aware of when dealing with litigation and your Solicitor.

An aspect of litigation which I find extremely perverse is that you go to a Solicitor to get advice, you have no idea if what you are being told is correct (or will win you the case), you have to pay for it and then take all the risks at the end of the day. The fact that you don't know what the return is going to be is bad enough – but what really gets me is that you are presented with a set of Terms and Conditions by your Solicitor which you have to sign up to which enables them to act, yet the average Client will be completely in the dark about what they are signing up to.

In those terms it will say *'we will do this'* and *'you must do that'* but, in my opinion, they are generally weighted in favour of the Solicitor. Most people will have no idea about what a Solicitor will be doing for them. You put yourself totally in their hands and have to trust them, as you sign your life away in some cases.

Let's face it, whatever your Solicitor advises you and whatever the outcome of your case, it is the Solicitor who will get paid irrespective of the result. If you lose it will effectively be a case of 'bad luck' but now you owe us £X,000! There is little or no risk for the Solicitor.

I personally believe that the average 'Client Care' letter (certainly from those I have seen) does not go far enough to protect a Client. Some letters can be so vaguely written that they can say enough just to get around the rules but they don't do what you need them to do: **clearly state what the Solicitor will be doing for you.** The odds can sometimes be stacked in favour of the Solicitor –

and I don't think that is right! I believe it is essential that a Client should redress the balance by turning the responsibility back on to the Solicitor.

How?

By creating 'Terms of Engagement' of your own which you must get your Solicitor to sign up to as well.

Why should your Solicitor be the only one to have their Terms and Conditions or Terms of Business signed?

Why should you sign them if they do not meet your requirements? After all, you are the customer and you are the one paying them.

Moreover, how do you know if what you are signing up to is going to meet your requirements when you don't even know what your requirements actually are? At the beginning of the case you will be 'in the dark' in terms of what to expect.

Your Terms of Engagement

I have provided a template of 'Terms of Engagement' which you can use to bind your Solicitor to act for you in the way that you want. You can use these as they stand or you can amend them to suit your own situation. They should be used to remove any grey areas where confusion may otherwise occur between what a Solicitor is required to do for you and your own personal expectations. In effect, these terms are an official statement of your objectives and requirements which you will ask your Solicitor to meet by signing up to them. They should thank you because the terms are doing part of their job for them (because they have to find out what your objectives are to meet the requirements of their Regulator).

I must stress that the draft Terms of Engagement document in this book contains nothing which any reasonable Solicitor should object to or be unwilling to sign up to.

If you find that a Solicitor is unwilling to sign these terms then you should ask yourself why. Although, depending on the nature of your case, it may be necessary to refine some of the terms to suit the situation – but don't give in on any of the terms unless you are absolutely happy to do so.

If they don't want to sign them, you may well have discovered in advance that they are not the Solicitors for you. You may find that some Solicitors will want to have one Agreement in place. If that is the case then you should simply ask that your Terms of Engagement are incorporated into their Terms of Business by the firm.

You may find that some Solicitors may not want to agree to the clause on 'Time Limitations'. This is a clause which relates to the time period for having your legal bills assessed (or an issue investigated). Personally, I do not see why any reasonable and fair-minded Solicitor should object to this, for the simple reason that if the Solicitor does their job properly, they should have nothing to fear. However, as I have said earlier in this book, if the Solicitor refuses to agree to waive the time limitations (and refuses to allow a Court to examine the bill) then at least you have been warned to check every bill you receive when it arrives. If you have any queries relating to it, raise these by notifying the Solicitor in writing and request a written explanation.

Obviously, the Solicitor agreeing to all these terms cannot be guaranteed for the reasons set out above. However, as I have said, if a Solicitor does not want to sign up to them, this could speak volumes about their true attitude and the real professional approach of that firm of Solicitors.

How to present the Terms of Engagement

You can either present these terms as part of a letter you write to your Solicitor at the outset or you can write a shorter covering letter and attach the Terms to it. Either way, you *must* ask your Solicitor to sign the document. If the Solicitor is going to act for you on a 'no win, no fee' basis then you will not need to use these Terms of Engagement. However, if the Solicitor is going to act for you and charge fees then you should seriously consider using the Terms of Engagement.

In most situations, the best way to present the Terms of Engagement is via the shorter covering letter with the Terms attached. For example, you could write your covering letter along the following lines:

ABC Solicitor
ABC House
ABC Road
ABC Town etc

Dear X,

Statement of my Requirements – Terms of Engagement

I refer to my decision to have you act on my behalf in connection with the XYZ case.

*I write to confirm my instructions and my requirements on how I wish matters to be dealt with. Accordingly, I enclose a mandate which sets out those requirements. These take the form of **Terms of Engagement** which will run in conjunction with the terms of your own firm. Before I sign up to the terms of your firm I would request that you also sign up to mine.*

Upon receipt of the signed terms, I will regard you as acting for me and I will sign your terms, if they are to my satisfaction. Alternatively, you may prefer to incorporate my terms into your own to form one agreement.

The enclosed terms are designed to bolster the terms your firm produces. In effect, signing my terms will further protect both parties from any misunderstandings while you act for me.

I thank you for your attention to this.

Yours sincerely,
(Client)

You can copy the Terms of Engagement overleaf (i.e. by scanning the pages or photocopying them – I would advise that, if you photocopy the pages, you should enlarge them by 144% to make them fit better onto A4 paper.

TERMS OF ENGAGEMENT

These Terms are provided to clarify the basis upon which the Client requires the Solicitor to act. The document records the Terms of Engagement on which all work is to be undertaken by your firm on behalf of the Client.

SRA/Law Society Rules and Codes

The Solicitor will adhere to the rules, codes and principles of The Law Society/SRA as a minimum standard when acting for the Client. Failure to do so will constitute a breach of the retainer.

Advice provided to Client

All advice provided to the Client will be in writing. Any verbal advice shall be followed up with written confirmation at the earliest opportunity. Advice constitutes any aspect, including cost estimates, risk assessment and legal advice in general. *The Solicitor will note that all advice, including cost estimates, will be relied upon by the Client throughout the case.*

Experience to act

The Client understands that the individual at the firm is held out as a Solicitor who has the requisite experience to act in the Client's case. If this is not true, or the Solicitor feels that they do not have the expertise to conduct the case in the required manner, then they must remove themselves and return all fees paid as well as pay the fees of the opponent incurred to that point.

Opponent's Ability to Pay

The Solicitor will take reasonable steps to check and verify that the opponent in the case is able to afford the costs if the Client wins the case. If no steps are taken to do this, and the opponent/s cannot pay, then the Solicitor will reimburse the Client for all fees incurred.

<u>Fees</u>

The Solicitor will provide accurate advice on all fees to be charged. In particular, the Solicitor *will*:

1. Provide an overall estimate of fees **across a range of possible outcomes** at the *outset* of the matter – to include Solicitor's costs, disbursements and VAT. The Client requires the Solicitor to be able to provide these estimates as well as providing estimates for the opponent's costs. The estimates therefore should be for 'global' amounts, *including the costs of an appeal and the costs of having the final bills assessed by Taxation*. The Solicitor will not wait until the 'Cost Budgeting' stage of any action before an overall estimate is provided for costs.

2. Give separate precise fee quotes for each phase of the matter (for Solicitor's costs, disbursements and VAT).

3. Give the Client the option of fixing the fees at a set overall amount for the entire case.

4. Not charge hourly fees more than the professional fee grade applicable to the person's experience/qualifications doing the work.

5. Not charge fees for other members of their staff doing work on the files without the express consent of the Client. Failure to notify and seek permission from the Client will render that portion of the fees 'not payable'.

6. Not charge the Client time for educating any member of their staff while working on the case.

7. Not include the Client's fees as part of any 'fee target' imposed by the firm. The fees charged are to be only for work done on the case that is reasonable and justified.

8. The Client will not be liable for any fees for work carried out on a specific task unless an estimate for that task has been provided to the Client (and the Client has agreed to it). For example, fees from Counsel for drafting a claim. Each task or stage must be broken down in a fee estimate.

9. The Client will not be charged multiple units of time for carrying out the same task by the Solicitor.

Advice on Cost Risk Benefit Analysis

The Solicitor will advise the Client properly on the costs, risks and benefits of the proposed action being taken. In particular, the Solicitor will:

1. Calculate the likely damages figure at the outset of the matter.

2. Carry out a cost risk benefit analysis.

3. Advise the Client if the action is worth pursuing or not in light of the above – including establishing if the opponent has sufficient funds to pay the costs/damages before committing the Client to the action.

4. Provide advice on the chances of success expressed in percentage terms and keep the Client updated should the percentages change (using Counsel if the case is complex enough to warrant this).

5. If the Solicitor fails to calculate damages properly and it transpires that the level of damages estimate was inaccurate (or unrealistic) and the Client is left out of pocket, then the Solicitor will compensate the Client for the wasted fees of the action (as well as the opponent's legal costs should the action fail).

Insurance

The Solicitor will take steps to obtain after-the-event insurance for the Client's case as soon as possible and report back to the Client on the outcome of the exploration exercise. The Client wishes to clarify that obtaining such insurance is important as it will assist in the ultimate decision on whether or not to proceed with the action.

Funding of the action

The Solicitor will seek to explore the possibility of and (if possible) obtain funding from a specialist legal fees lender, secured against any after-the-event insurance policy which the Solicitor arranges.

Inaccurate fees or exceeding estimates

If the fees charged exceed the estimates provided, the Client will not pay the Solicitor the fees over and above the estimates (unless the Client has previously agreed in writing). The Solicitor will not terminate the retainer if the fees are exceeded and the Client does not pay the extra. The Solicitor will therefore finish the case they have started and not come off the record because of a fee dispute in these circumstances. The Solicitor will proceed with the case to a conclusion at trial, and beyond, if necessary.

Informing the Client of all material facts

The Solicitor will inform the Client of all material facts relating to the case, including advice from Counsel and any other matter which may arise.

Supplying the Client with ongoing information

The Solicitor will send the Client copies of:

1. All attendance notes (including meetings, internal memos and telephone calls) from day one and as and when they occur on an ongoing basis throughout the case.

2. All letters, faxes and emails sent and received to the opponent or third parties, from day one and as and when they are sent or received.

Passing of Client's instructions to Counsel

The Solicitor will pass all instructions specifically for Counsel from the Client to Counsel.

Removing documents from the Client's premises

If the Solicitor removes any files or documents from the Client's premises for the purposes of the case, the Solicitor will send an inventory of the files/documents removed and be responsible for their safe keeping. The Solicitor will copy the files/documents and return the original files/documents to the Client within 7 days. Alternatively, if the Solicitor needs to keep the original files/documents, they will copy the said documents and send these copies to the Client. If the Solicitor loses any files or documents they will compensate the Client accordingly.

In the event that the Solicitor changes firms

In the event that the Solicitor handling the Client's case moves to another firm, the firm will not charge the Client for the time a replacement Solicitor takes to read into the file. If the original Solicitor moves to another firm, the Client will deem this to be an unsatisfactory disruption to the effective management of the case. Whilst the Client accepts that movement between Solicitor firms occurs from time to time within the profession, the Client reserves the right to maintain the services of the original Solicitor, even if they move to another firm. However, if the Solicitor moves to another firm then the Terms of Engagement must be honoured by the new firm. If the new firm does not honour any aspect of these terms then the original firm of Solicitors will be bound to honour any aspect which the new firm does not. Alternatively, when the Solicitor moves to the new firm and presents the new 'Client Care' letter, they will sign these Terms of Engagement again.

Charging time for rectifying errors/oversights

If the Solicitor makes any error and that mistake causes further work to be done to rectify/resolve the problem caused, the Solicitor will not charge the Client for their time in rectifying the matter. Likewise, the Solicitor will not charge the Client for the time taken to investigate/respond to a complaint about the Solicitor's service or charges.

Time Limitations

The Solicitor agrees to waive all time limitations on any aspect of the assessment of any of the bills (i.e. the 12 month limitation) or the time period for an investigation by the Legal Ombudsman/The Law Society of any aspect of the service provided by the Solicitor or their conduct. The Solicitor agrees to their bills being subject to 'Cost Assessment' by a Court if the Client wishes to apply for the assessment within a 6 year period from the bill being sent. The Solicitor agrees to be bound by the findings of the Court in that assessment process and agrees to waiving the 12 month time limit.

Termination

The Client may terminate the retainer at any time, giving notice to the Solicitor in writing.

For the Client   **For the Solicitor**

Signed: ....   Signed: ....

Name: ....   Name: ....

Date: ....   Date: ....

Observations & Tips

- Being aware of the 12 month time limitation on having your Solicitor's bills assessed is very important. I know of someone (a pensioner) who was seriously overcharged by his firm of Solicitors over a period of several years in a litigation matter and the fee earner at the firm gave him all sorts of excuses over the course of those years to encourage him to pay as he went along (without giving him a detailed breakdown of what he was charging for). The person trusted the individual and paid the bills in good faith. However, when the true facts of the case came to light at a later date, the person complained. The firm's bills were looked at in detail by an independent Costs Draftsman and it was clear that he had been grossly overcharged (with evidence that the fee earner had loaded the bills and charged for things which he had assured the person he would not charge for as well as charging for meetings which never took place). When the firm was asked if they would agree to have all of his bills assessed before a Costs Judge, the firm refused using the 12 month time limitation as an excuse. The firm was acutely aware that it could not justify a considerable portion of the fees. The firm also knew it would be in trouble at a cost assessment hearing. Therefore, the firm was able to hide behind this rule contained in the Solicitor's Act and the firm got away with pocketing the person's hard earned money.

CHAPTER 12

Judgments given by Judges

(Judgments are not perfect or even always factually correct)

Everyone would like to think that, in most cases, the right decision is made by a Judge and justice will prevail. I am sorry to tell you that Judgments are not always entirely perfect or even correct.

Do not for one second assume that all Judgments handed down by Judges are always fair or accurately reflect the facts of a case (even if the decision goes for you or against you).

In most cases, a decision will be made entirely by a single Judge and depending on the Judge you get, the decision may go for you on the day or against you if a different Judge had presided over your case.

Perverse and unexplainable Judgments do get handed down by Judges as well as good ones. Ask any experienced Barrister or Q.C. or Solicitor how many cases they have seen over the years where a bizarre Judgment has been made or an unexplainable conclusion has been arrived that which did not fit with the facts of the case. Any experienced Lawyer will tell you that they have seen several in their time. If they say they have seen none, they have simply not been practising for very long!

Barristers and Judges seem to take up a lot of their time seeking to establish a 'legal line' and where that line exists, with each Barrister trying to argue where the line should be. Sadly, in all of the time given to hearing long and complex legal arguments, what often gets ignored is the simple 'truth' and common sense. Judges can even get basic facts wrong sometimes.

Sometimes, it is not the fault of the Judge but the fault of the Barrister in failing to put all of the facts before the Court. Therefore, the Judge is sometimes left with no choice but to make the decision they do because of the way the evidence was presented (or was not presented).

However, some Judges simply do occasionally make Judgments which are beyond explanation, common sense or logic even when the evidence is put before the Court. You do not just have to take my word for this. To illustrate the point, Lord Justice Ward in a case before the Court of Appeal was moved to openly criticise and register his disagreement of the position adopted by two fellow Lord Justices (and a Lord Justice Stanley Burnton in particular). The case was *Oceanbulk Shipping & Trading SA v TMT Asia Limited (2010) EWCA Civ 79*. In paragraph 41 of the Appeal Court Judgment, Lord Justice Ward said:

> "......... I am outnumbered, nay outgunned, by the commercial colossi seated either side of me. I prefer the instincts of the youthful Stanley Burnton J before he became corrupted by the arid atmosphere of this Court. It goes to prove what every good old-fashioned county court judge knows: the higher you go, the less the essential oxygen of common sense is available to you. So I am unrepentant..........."

And that's a Judge talking about another Judge!

You may also be interested to learn that the same Lord Justice Stanley Burnton was later publicly criticised by Lord Neuberger (the Master of the Rolls and a Head of the Judiciary at the time) for courting publicity when he chose to appear as an amateur food critic on a prime time TV cooking programme!

On the whole, you would like to think that Judges are generally fair and have the capacity to exercise good judgment. However, there are occasions where some Judges fall short and are sometimes guilty of poor judgment themselves. They are only human after all. In the same way that you should never automatically believe what you read in a newspaper article, you should think twice before believing everything you read in a Judgment.

Negligence cases against Solicitors

In looking at negligence cases against Solicitors, I have come to form the opinion that there really are some Solicitors, Barristers, Q.C.'s and Judges who just assume a Client exists for the convenience of the litigation profession itself. During the years I have been involved in litigation cases, I have seen Solicitors, Barristers, Q.C.'s (and Judges) who simply do not properly understand how Solicitors are supposed to act to protect the interests of a Client (especially in relation to cost/risk/benefit and overall level of fees charged by a Solicitor). These representatives of the litigation profession seem oblivious to the plight of the Client and have never stopped to consider the true extent of the Client's interests.

Some Judges just think that a Client should have no complaint when a Solicitor overcharges them or has a service issue (as if it is just something which a Client should expect when they use a Solicitor).

To me, the reason for their ignorance stems from inadequate education and training when they joined the profession in the first place. For example, some Judges may start off as Barristers (or even Solicitors) and work their way up to becoming High Court Judges. However, if some of them haven't learned the basics at the outset it can lead to ignorance and the wrong 'mind-set' later in their careers – especially relevant if they become a Judge. It seems to me that some Solicitors, Barristers, Q.C.'s and Judges get themselves qualified and hit the profession running to get on the fee earning 'gravy train' without ever stopping to properly learn the rules of the relevant regulators. They literally start to 'run before they can walk' in the belief that they are entitled to just charge a Client fees because they are somehow worthy through qualification.

Accordingly, some Judges have probably led very sheltered lives and would do well to acquaint themselves with the realities of life which members of the public face.

An additional risk you face is that a Judge allocated to your case will not necessarily have a proper awareness of the subject matter of your case (especially important if it is a technical one or to do with a professional matter - i.e. in cases of Solicitor's negligence). And herein lies another imperfection and weakness in the legal system. The system cannot guarantee that you will get a Judge with the necessary detailed knowledge of the subject matter of your case.

I regularly ask myself this question:

How many Solicitors, Barristers or Judges truly and properly know the Codes of Conduct of the SRA/Law Society and know how they should be applied?

Answer: Not as many as you might expect.

I bet if you asked all the Solicitors practising today what the practice rules were and asked them to explain the principles of each one, only a handful would be able to do it.

Is that good enough?

I don't think so.

Also, I bet if you asked all the Judges presiding in Courts today what the practice rules were, you would find that few Judges would be aware of these (and even if they were aware, how many of these Judges would ever apply the rules in a real life case before their Court?).

Judges - they need to be monitored and assessed themselves

Having seen first hand how Judges can sometimes get things wrong and make mistakes, I truly believe that a system needs to be introduced whereby Judges are constantly assessed for performance, medical fitness and fairness.

I believe that a regulatory body should be set up within the Judiciary to monitor them and Judges should be required to prove their fitness to judge and be subject to assessment throughout their careers on the quality of the decisions they make.

Barristers should participate in the assessment process by reporting their opinions on how Judges perform after each case has concluded.

I also believe that a task force of independent assessors within the regulatory body should travel around the Courts of the country to assess the performance and conduct of Judges. Some Judges do not conduct themselves in a way becoming of their position in society – some can be rude, arrogant and sarcastic.

Judges should also be required to disclose to the regulatory body what medication they are taking at any one point in time as well as disclosing their weekly consumption of alcohol. This may sound extreme but it really is not because it is simple common sense. I say this because many Judges are well advanced in age.

My other concern is that, how do you know if some Judges are on medication or not? i.e. whether it is for blood pressure regulation or cholesterol reduction or the like. What if some of them have personal problems such as depression? They may also be on medication for that. These drugs can have an adverse effect on the mind's ability to think and function. As the primary purpose of a Judge is to use their mind to make decisions, the importance of such monitoring cannot be overestimated.

In addition, what do we know of the personal lives of the Judges?

Some Judges may be going through personal problems of their own which can affect their ability to think and concentrate properly. For example, just speaking to people locally where I live, it is common knowledge that one Judge was known to openly speak of the cases he was presiding over during discussions with people in a pub, openly making a joke of the witnesses concerned based on the clothes they were wearing. The Judge once openly declared in the pub that he was going to find against an individual because he did not like the jacket he had worn when he gave his evidence in the witness box!

The same Judge was also known to mow his lawn at the weekend wearing his wife's dresses!

Another Judge I heard about went sex crazy after having a vasectomy. His wife divorced him because she could not take his sexual demands. She drew the line at having to cover herself in chocolate every time he wanted sex! He became obsessed with chasing women and cheated on his wife.

Another Judge was known to physically assault his wife and children and behaved in a generally foul manner towards them.

I mention the above because I regularly ask myself this question: if a Judge thinks it is appropriate to behave in such an inappropriate manner in their own personal life (whether it be towards other human beings or just their own behaviour in general), what is that Judge doing being allowed to preside over cases where their decisions and their own belief process can adversely affect other people who are more decent human beings than themselves?

What standards of behaviour are those Judges using to arrive at conclusions in legal cases?

How do you really know the true character of a Judge who might be appointed to your case?

You don't.

Annual medical checks for Judges

I believe that all Judges should be required to undergo annual medical checks to detect for brain damage from strokes. I am being deadly serious.

A stroke can damage the brain's ability to function. Having learned a great deal about strokes from my father's own experience and talking to his medical specialists, you would be amazed at the number of people who have suffered strokes and do not realise they have experienced one. On the outside, these individuals might appear normal but if they have suffered any kind of stroke their brain will be damaged because blood vessels die in the brain when a stroke occurs and their ability to think and reason can be seriously impaired.

Judges are not immune to strokes and it is essential that a system is in place to continuously assess them. At the very least, all Judges over the age of 60 should have to undergo a compulsory annual brain scan.

I truly believe that all Judges should be subject to regular cognitive (brain function) testing. I bet that if all the Judges in the UK were subject to cognitive testing tomorrow, the general public (and the Judiciary) would be surprised at the varying results of their brain functions.

Such testing would identify which Judges are not fit to remain in their positions as a result of impaired brain function. This would also introduce a new natural selection process whereby fresh and younger brains would replace the old guard when they are no longer fit to be Judges.

At present, a quite serious shortcoming exists within the Judiciary because it does not appear to have any formal process in place to assess Judges and identify when a Judge should be retired. Regular cognitive testing for Judges would address this problem.

Register of Judges interests

Judges should also be required to formally register their interests with the regulatory body (e.g. memberships of clubs, their associations with organisations and charities etc). Details of their interests should be made available to the public to ensure transparency.

When such a great deal is at stake for Claimants and Defendants in litigation matters, it is only right and proper that Judges are fit (and are seen to be fit) to hold the positions of responsibility they do. Judges have the power to seriously affect people's lives by the decisions they make and they should be monitored on their fitness to do their job. The legal profession seems to regard Judges as untouchable. They should not be.

When all is said and done, Judges are public servants with their salaries and pensions funded by the tax-payer. Why shouldn't they be subject to this scrutiny?

The process of cross-examination in Court is a very unnatural process which causes normal human beings to behave in an abnormal way. Accordingly, no Judge should draw conclusions solely related to the answers given by a witness or their demeanour.

Personally, I believe the cross-examination process in a Court room should be scrapped. The process should be replaced by a more informal approach where questions are posed around a table (like a mediation) where people can see the whites of each other's eyes and can speak to each other on the same level, with the Judge sitting at the table. Of course, no process is going to be 100% perfect but this would be a much fairer and more calming process where each witness has the best chance of doing the best for themselves.

Some Judges make unfair assumptions based on a person's demeanour in a witness box and use these to draw conclusions and underpin the decision they want to make.

In most cases, a Judge will make a decision on how they wish to find on a case and then paint a picture in their Judgment, where they create a story using their own version of the characters in the case to fit the conclusions of their tale. Judges can create their own version of the facts, based on nothing more than guesswork or deliberate manipulation of those facts to bolster what they want to say.

Having seen first hand what can happen in Court, I will never read any Judgment and believe 100% what the Judge has written. There will always be a nagging doubt in my mind that it is possibly a 'stitch-up', manufactured by a Judge to fit the decision he or she wanted to give, rather than a properly analysed representation of the facts. I would advise everyone to be equally sceptical when reading Judgments themselves. They are not necessarily works of authenticity or reliability.

144

When you see the phrase "*Mr X was not a reliable witness*", you should not automatically interpret this to mean that Mr X was not telling the truth. This is a typical phrase a Judge may use to simply (and conveniently) pour cold water on evidence they do not want to accept because it does not fit with the decision the Judge wants to make. Indeed, I have seen people giving evidence in Court when I know for a fact they were telling the truth. However, the Judge chose not to believe them. I have also seen people give evidence when I know they were lying – yet the Judge chose to believe their story because it suited the decision the Judge wanted to make. There are always two sides to every story.

You should not automatically accept one person's view and their explanation for holding that view, even if it is written in a formal Judgment.

What can also be very disheartening is, when the Judgment comes out, you see third parties latch on to the Judge's comments as if they have come from a 'super oracle of truth'. It is all rather sad and a reflection of how shoddy and flawed the judicial process can be. Sometimes the Judge's comments are not always supported by the facts when analysed properly.

For all the clever legal arguments put forward by legal representatives, for all the money these people charge and for all the faith you want to place in the Judge and the judicial process, there is a chance that the Judgment itself will turn out to be a load of twaddle!

Humans are not perfect and you soon realise that those working in the legal profession, whether they are Judges, Barristers or Solicitors, are as fallible as any other person walking this planet. In reality, the judicial process does not always provide justice or accuracy of fact when it comes to decision making.

The mis-use of the word 'Justice'

A final observation I would make in this chapter concerns the naming of Courts in general and how the word 'justice' is portrayed to the public.

For example, the High Court is often referred to as the *'Royal Courts of Justice'* (RCJ for short). I have also seen other Courts in the UK which have official signs on the side of the buildings saying *'Courts of Justice'*. However, the reference to the word 'justice' is quite misleading.

To most people like you and me, the word 'justice' means to be treated fairly and seeing the right and proper outcome achieved. The Oxford Dictionary defines 'justice' as *'just conduct; fairness; exercise of authority in maintenance of right'*.

The use of the word 'justice' to describe a building (which is part of a Court service) gives the impression that the Court is a place where people go and receive justice as a guaranteed outcome. How the Court Service is allowed to use the word 'justice' is surprising.

Quite honestly, I don't understand why the Court Service has not been taken to task under the ***'Trades Descriptions Act 1968'*** for promoting itself as a service provider where people can go to get 'justice'. It simply cannot guarantee that justice will prevail in any Court case. I personally think that all Courts should be re-named the *'Courts for the Pursuit of Justice (with no guarantee that you will actually get it)'*.

Or better still, simply re-name all Court buildings and their descriptions to *'Courts of Justice (and Injustice)'*. That would be a much more accurate and balanced description. Or even better, just stick to using a sign which says *'Court'*!

In that way, more people will appreciate the imperfections of the legal system and that absolutely nothing is certain, despite what the law (and some of those who practice within it) may suggest.

So, be warned! When you take a case to Court, the information contained in this chapter is something which you should be aware of.

CHAPTER 13

To proceed or not to proceed? … That is the question.

The 'C.R.A.P.' Principle

I hope this book has helped you appreciate what can happen in litigation and potential difficulties which can arise. I also hope that it will help you navigate a course around some of those difficulties.

Litigation really is a lottery and you need to think carefully before buying your ticket to play or not. Getting involved with Lawyers and the legal system can be like dancing with the devil. I would even go further by saying that Solicitors should be required by law to put a warning on top of their printed letterhead (as you see on cigarette packets) saying:

WARNING
LITIGATION CAN SERIOUSLY DAMAGE
YOUR HEALTH AND WEALTH

Obviously, I can't tell you whether to proceed with your case or not because that decision is yours. Your decision will be influenced by the details of your case, your situation and the advice of your legal representatives – but from my own experience and research amongst other people who have been there before, I can give you advice to help you make your final decision.

Unless you have managed to secure 'after-the-event' insurance, if you have a legal action to pursue (or defend), you should consider looking at it this way: project yourself ahead to the end of the case where you may have lost. Think of all the money it has cost you. Use the *TCF Principle* to work it out.

Are you able to live with that?

Is the case really that important?

Are you able to live with the financial loss, the stress and nausea as well as the lost opportunities to do other more productive things with your time?

Having lost the case, given the chance of going back in time, would you have preferred to have kept your money in your pocket and let the action drop (or settle it)?

If the answer is *"I can live with the prospect of losing"*, then you may feel inclined to continue with your action. If the case is really important to you or unavoidable then you will no doubt wish to go ahead.

If you say to yourself *"No, I can't live with the thought of losing all the money"*, then don't bother with the action (or if you are defending an action then settle it as soon as possible to minimise further costs).

Let me tell you this, there is absolutely nothing wrong in letting an action drop or settling, if that's what you feel is best. It is far better to take stock and enjoy what you already have, and live your life instead. It is better to have a life than have it ruined by avoidable litigation – which would otherwise only enhance the standard of living of your Solicitor.

Do remember that a Solicitor, no matter how good they are, should tell you that they cannot be certain what the outcome of the case will be (unless it is a simple and straightforward matter). In fact, a Solicitor's job is all about 'uncertainty'. In reality, a Solicitor's job is about managing uncertainty. Solicitors usually take no risk while everything is uncertain for their Clients. The only certainty is that they will want to be paid.

Of course, if you have a case which you have no option but to pursue or defend, then going ahead is almost a foregone conclusion. However, if you do proceed, then *please* make sure that your Solicitor acts in your best interests from day one and conducts the matter according to the methods outlined in this book as a *minimum* standard.

If you don't go ahead with the action, that's fine. If you do, then go and buy that diary and notebook **NOW** to keep a record of the advice you receive and the costs. Get a copy made of the 'Terms of Engagement' and get your Solicitor to sign it.

The C.R.A.P. Principle

To simplify the decision even further, my own personal theory for those of you trying to decide whether to proceed with litigation or not, is that you should use the **C.R.A.P.** principle.

Ironic though the use of these letters is, and what the letters spell, this is not a cheap attempt to be crude. Appropriate though the word may be to describe the whole legal experience for some, it is a simple principle which cuts through all the technical and legal jargon and dilemmas which may otherwise play on your mind and complicate your decision. Put all these complications to one side and use this 4 point principle. It is very easy to remember. Think **C.R.A.P.** and follow this:

> **C** ost?
> **R** isk?
> **A** ssess?
> **P** roceed (or not)?

You simply need to say to yourself: What is the cost if I lose? What are the risks? Then you need to assess the situation and then decide whether to proceed or not. A good Solicitor should work to this principle as a matter of course because their duty to you is concerned with identifying and advising on costs and risks.

I am deadly serious. Keep this principle in mind when you are sitting in that meeting with Counsel or with your Solicitor. Keep this principle in mind when you are on the phone speaking to your Solicitor or when reading one of his/her letters. Keep this principle in mind when they are bombarding you with legal theories and arguments about your case. Keep thinking **C.R.A.P.** Hopefully, the advice you receive from them will not turn out to crap in itself!

A final thought

I will round off the book by leaving you with a sobering comment which a Barrister told me. In his opinion, he said that cases are rarely won on the law or the facts. According to him, cases are won on 'merit' and how matters unfold on the day in Court. A Judge will look at each party's case and decide which one he or she prefers. A Judge will simply fit the law and the facts to match the decision he or she wants to make.

Having experience myself, and from talking to other lay-people as well as legal professionals, there are two schools of thought on the Barrister's theory. On the one hand, yes. The statement is true in many cases. Whatever anyone believes, the only thing that is certain is that nothing is certain in litigation.

So, if you decide not to proceed, take strength from the fact that you have saved yourself a great deal of money, time and stress. You've just taken the decision not to participate in a lottery.

If you do go ahead, then I wish you the best of luck and every success. I hope you get the right Judge on the right day - and a damn good Solicitor!

If I had one simple message to give to all Solicitors, it would be to have the professionalism and guts to tell the Client at the earliest possible stage what the total costs might be for the entire case. If a Client is told how much he or she is potentially going to lose overall, at least they can decide for themselves whether they wish to pursue the case or not (rather than the Client finding out when it is too late).

Observations & Tips

- If you decide to go ahead with your action (or defend it), then go to the SRA/The Law Society website (or call them) and obtain a full copy of the SRA Code of Conduct/Practice Rules. These are the rules which apply to the way your Solicitor conducts your case. The rules are varied from time to time so that is why it is a good idea to get hold of the rules applicable at the time your case begins. The rules are set out in a very clear manner and are easy to follow.

- Don't be afraid to quote specific SRA Codes/Law Society rules when dealing with your Solicitor – it will send the message that you know what you are talking about and you won't be messed with. You might even teach your Solicitor something they don't know.

- Never make a crusade out of any situation using the legal profession (unless you can afford it).

- Remember, it's not all over when the case ends – you have got all the costs arguments to come and there's no guarantee when or if you will receive money from your opponent.

- If you lose the case, your Solicitor may probably tell you to be philosophical about it and accept it. Bear in mind that they probably were not saying that when they were taking your money and telling you that you had a good chance of winning!

- Remember, if an insurance company won't take the risk on your case then why should you? An insurer's refusal to offer 'after-the-event' insurance for you may be an indication that your case isn't as good as you imagine (or not as good as you have been led to believe).

CHAPTER 14

What if you are unable to afford to pay for the services of a Solicitor or Legal Representation?

If you are unable to afford to pay for the services of a Solicitor in England or Wales (either because you have no money in the first place or your Solicitor has left you high and dry as a result of a disagreement over your case or fees etc), there are further options available for you to explore. There is no guarantee that you will obtain assistance but they are worth a try. Here is a simplified check list:

- Have you checked to see if your case is covered by your household insurance policy or business insurance policy under legal expenses cover?

- If not covered, have you checked to see if you are eligible for Public Funding (also called Legal Aid)? You can check with a Solicitor or call the **Community Legal Service** on 0845 345 4 345 for further guidance. You can also try your local **Citizens Advice Bureau** (*www.citizensadvice.org.uk*).

- You could also try **Advice UK** on 0207 469 5700. They might be able to give you some general legal advice and also inform you of the nearest Advice UK centre where you can visit.

- If not, have you checked with another Solicitor to see if they can take your case on a "no win, no fee" basis?

- If not, have you considered making an application for assistance from a Pro Bono Solicitor via **LawWorks** at The National Pro Bono Centre, 48 Chancery Lane, London WC2A IJF. Contact 0207 092 3940 (or at *enquiries@lawworks.org.uk*).

- If necessary, also consider making an application for Pro Bono assistance from a Barrister via the **Bar Pro Bono Unit** at The National Pro Bono

Centre, 48 Chancery Lane, London WC2A IJF. Contact 0207 092 3960 (or at *enquiries @barprobono.org.uk*).

- If that is not possible, consider contacting the **Law Centres Network** at *www.lawcentres.org.uk*. Law Centres offer legal advice, casework and representation to individuals and groups who cannot afford to pay for legal advice. The network can help you find a Law Centre which might be able to assist. The Law Centres Network can also be contacted at Floor 1, Tavis House, 1-6 Tavistock Square, London WC1H 9NA. Contact telephone number: (020) 3637 1330.

GLOSSARY OF TERMS

This Glossary of Terms is provided to help you understand some of the language and terminology used in civil litigation. The Glossary is not supposed to be totally comprehensive and does not set out to include definitions of every single legal term or phrase. The definitions included here are put together from the words and phrases I came across during my experiences with litigation.

Admitted
The term 'admitted' means that an individual has been admitted to practice as a Solicitor by the Master of the Roles. An individual has to be admitted in order to call themselves a Solicitor. They also have to hold a valid Practice Certificate from The Law Society (unless they are exempt in some cases).

Advocate
A term to describe a person who pleads for another in Court. For example, a Barrister is an advocate because he or she will plead your case in Court. You can also find Solicitors who have the right to act as advocates too.

Affidavit
A document which certifies the facts by a witness. It is a sworn statement made by an individual, swearing that the contents of the documents are true and correct (to the best of the knowledge of the person making the affidavit).

After-the-Event Insurance
An insurance policy which covers the costs of your opponent in the event that you lose the case.

Allocation
The process by which the judicial system allocates a case to a particular means of dealing with it within the Court system. For example, a small claims case may be allocated to the 'small claims track'. A bigger case may be allocated to the 'multi-track' or the 'fast-track' Court route. It is all to do with how the case will be managed through the Court system.

Allocation Directions

The directions (i.e. instructions) made by the Court at the allocation stage of the litigation – i.e. when the case is to be allocated to a particular track such as a small claims track, multi-track or fast-track route. The directions will depend on the type of case and its circumstances. The directions are normally made by a Judge following receipt of the 'Allocation Questionnaires' from both parties. The directions enable the judicial system to assign the most appropriate Court resources for dealing with the dispute (having regard to the size of the financial claims and other considerations).

Allocation Questionnaire (also referred to as 'Directions Questionnaire')

A document issued to each party in the litigation which has to be submitted to the Court for allocation purposes (it is usually not issued until all of the Defences in the litigation are filed). The document requires questions to be answered by both sides to enable the Court to properly understand the case. The document is filed and served by both parties and will include details of estimated costs, value of claim, nature of remedy of being sought, complexity of facts, number of parties involved and number of witnesses and so on. A Client should also receive a copy of the allocation questionnaires from their Solicitor.

Alternative Dispute Resolution (ADR)

A means of resolving a dispute or legal action. ADR is an alternative means of resolving an action than at a trial in Court. This usually takes the form of a 'mediation' between the parties, depending on the nature of the action being sought. Other options include 'conciliation' or 'negotiation'. A third party plays a central role in resolving the dispute by assisting the parties. The parties are usually free to walk away from the proceedings and continue with litigation if they wish. The Courts encourage all disputes to be resolved by ADR before a full blown trial occurs.

Appeal

A legal procedure to a higher Court to argue that a judgment in a lower Court is wrong on an issue of law. Appeals are usually restricted both on 'grounds' of the appeal and 'time-limits' for when an appeal can be lodged.

Arbitration

The settling of a dispute by an arbitrator. The arbitrator acts as a third party. Arbitration is an alternative to litigation which involves an arbitrator reaching a judgment – the judgment of the arbitrator is binding for both parties. The decision is known as an 'award'.

Assessment

A term used for assessing legal costs. It is sometimes referred to as 'Taxation'. The assessment process is carried out by a Costs Judge who will go through the bills to check if they are fair and reasonable. This normally takes place after the case has ended if the parties cannot agree the overall costs.

Attendance Note

A note made by your Solicitor on the file which relates to any situation where they have 'attended to' your case. For example, writing up a note of a meeting or telephone call.

Bar

A historical term which comes from the short wall (or divide) in Court rooms which separates the Judges from the body of the Court. A Q.C. addresses the Judge from within the Bar. A Junior Barrister addresses the Judge at the Bar (and outside). The term Bar is also used when describing Barristers or Q.C.'s. For example, a person becomes a Barrister when they are 'called to the Bar'. The term is also used to describe a section of the legal profession.

Bar Council

The approved Regulator of the Bar of England and Wales. The organisation regulates Barristers and discharges its regulatory functions through the independent **Bar Standards Board**.

Bar Pro Bono Unit

A charitable operation which helps find free legal assistance from volunteer Barristers for those who cannot afford to pay. Assistance from the unit must be applied for through either a Solicitor or Advice Agency (i.e. Citizen's Advice Bureau or Law Centre). Further details can be found at *www.barprobono.org.uk* or at 'Bar Pro Bono Unit', The National Pro

Bono Centre, 48 Chancery Lane, London WC2A 1JF. Telephone 0207 092 3960. PLEASE BEAR IN MIND THE UNIT IS A CHARITABLE ORGANISATION AND HAS LIMITED RESOURCES. THE WORK WHICH THE UNIT CARRIES OUT IS INVALUABLE TO THE PEOPLE IT HELPS. THE UNIT IS GRATEFUL FOR CHARITABLE DONATIONS.

Barrister

A Barrister is someone who has been admitted to 'the bar' and is permitted to appear in Court to argue a Client's case.

Breach

The breaking (or neglect) of a law, promise or duty.

Brief

The process by which a Solicitor instructs a Barrister or Q.C. to appear as an advocate in Court.

Brief Fee

The fee charged by a Barrister or Q.C. for the brief (above). The brief fee is a charge for preparing the case and appearing at Court. An additional daily fee will be charged for each day spent in Court at the trial (this is known as a 'refresher' fee).

Case Law

Law established by previous Judgments.

Case Management Conference (CMC)

An informal meeting between representatives of the parties in an action and a Judge, usually held in a Court. The purpose of such meetings/conferences is to establish 'directions' for the case (like when the deadlines for witness statements exchange are to be, date for disclosure of documents, trial hearing date etc.). The purpose of CMC's is to keep cases on track and on time so that they can progress through the Court system as swiftly as possible. The meetings can take place in open Court or in a meeting room or even via a conference telephone call.

Causation (in a civil matter)

The act or process which causes something to happen or exist. It is a 'cause and effect' relationship between the act (or omission) and damages alleged as a result. Normally, the first question which would need to be asked is: *would the current situation or circumstances be different, had the act or omission not occurred?* The general test for causation is the 'but for' test which requires a Claimant to show that the injury or damage would not have occurred but for the negligence of the Defendant (i.e. causation exists when the result would not have occurred without the Defendant's negligence).

Chancery Division
See under 'High Court' .

Circuit Judge (Civil)
A full time Judge who deals solely in civil and family work and divides their time between these. They may specialise in a particular area of the law. Circuit Judges generally hear claims worth over £15,000 or those involving greater complexity or importance.

Citizens Advice Bureau
Citizens Advice Bureaux (CAB) offer help and advice to the public on a range of issues. Offices are located throughout the country. They can deal with many different type of query (consumer queries, debit or repossession etc). The Bureau can refer you elsewhere if you have a more complicated problem (to a Solicitor, Law Centre or Legal Advice Centre) for assistance. Addresses of your local office can be found in your local telephone directory or at *www.citizensadvice.org.uk.* The CAB is a good place to try as a first port of call because they can refer you to other organisations which may be able to give you more detailed help.

Civil Procedure Rules (CPR)
The Civil Procedure Rules are rules which govern the procedure aspects of the conduct of legal proceedings in the UK.

Claim Form
A formal written statement which sets out the particulars of the Claimant, the Defendant and the remedy being sought under the legal proceedings.

Claimant
A person who commences legal proceedings in litigation.

Claimant (Part 20)
A Claimant who is a 'Defendant' to the legal proceedings in the beginning. This occurs when the person makes a 'counterclaim' to the action being taken against them. The 'counterclaim' is made under Part 20 of the CPR rules.

Clerk

An individual who assists Solicitors in the execution of their professional duties. They are sometimes called 'Legal Clerks' (as opposed to Barristers and Q.C.'s clerks who work at Counsel's chambers in an administrative capacity). If they are fee earners at the firm, then clerks are only able to charge a certain grade of fee (i.e. lower than a Solicitor). Their work must be supervised by a Solicitor at the firm.

Common Law

Law which is not part of legislation. It consists of rules of law based on common custom and reliance on Court decisions (i.e. 'case law').

Conditional Fee Arrangement

An arrangement whereby a Solicitor or Lawyer and the Client agree to share the risks of the litigation by coming to an arrangement on the fees payable, based on the result of the litigation. There are 2 types of CFA: (1) 'No Win, No Fee' and (2) 'Shared Risk' – please see Chapter 6.

Conflict of Interest

A situation where there is benefit to one person which might cause a disadvantage to another. Solicitors must avoid conflicts of interest unless openly declared and accepted.

Costs Budget

A budget of costs submitted to Court by parties in a litigation case. The Court will oversee the agreement to the budget. The parties (except litigants in person) must file and exchange budgets when filing the Allocation Questionnaires, or, if no date is specified for filing the questionnaire, at least 7 days before the first Case Management Conference. Costs Budgeting applies to Multi-Track cases. It does not apply in the Admiralty and Commercial Courts or if fixed costs or scale costs apply to the case. The consequences of failing to file a budget will mean that the party in default is deemed to have filed a budget comprising only the court fee.

Costs Capping Order

An Order made by a Court limiting the amount of future costs (including disbursements) which a party may recover.

Costs Draftsman

A specialist who assesses legal bills and is concerned with all aspects of Solicitor's costs. They can analyse bills, prepare points of dispute relating to the bills and make representations in Court on a Client's behalf.

Costs Management Conference

A hearing which is convened solely for the purpose of cost management (i.e. to approve a 'Costs Budget 'or a revised 'Costs Budget').

Cost Management Order

An order made by a Court which records the extent to which 'Costs Budgets' are agreed between parties. For budgets (or parts of budget) which are not agreed between the parties, the Court will record the Court's approval after making necessary revisions to the budgets. If a Cost Management Order has been made by a Court, the Court will thereafter have a greater control of the parties' budget in respect of recoverable costs payable to the winning party by the losing party.

Counterclaim

A claim made by a Defendant in response to a Claimant's claim. Counterclaims are usually made in conjunction with a defence in the proceedings.

County Court

Courts which deal with most cases. The High Court is reserved for high calibre cases, public law cases and some specialist matters.

Court of Appeal

The Court which hears appeals from all divisions of the High Court (and in some instances County Courts and some Tribunals). The Civil Division is presided over by The Master of the Rolls. An appeal is granted subject to obtaining the requisite permission.

Court of Session

[Scottish Law] The highest civil Court in Scotland. It has an 'Outer House' which deals with cases initially before any appeal. It then has an 'Inner House' which deals with appeals. The principal Judge is the Lord President.

Damages

Monetary award made by a Court to an injured party to be paid by another party.

Default Judgment

A judgment given when a Defendant fails to serve an acknowledgment of service or a defence to a claim within the statutory timescales. A judgment may be applied for if this occurs.

Defendant

A person against whom legal proceedings are taken in a Court.

Deputy District Judge

A Judge appointed to sit at the County Court to manage and try civil, family, costs, enforcement and insolvency cases. They try small-claims and fast-track cases as well as making procedural directions to prepare cases for trial. Their jurisdiction is broadly similar to full-time District Judges although they have limited authority in some instances. They are not full-time and the post is open to any qualified Solicitor or Barrister with at least 7 years experience.

Directions

Instructions given by Judges in Court to make sure cases adhere to the necessary timescales and deadlines in order to bring the case to Court.

Disbursements

Fees incurred by a Solicitor other than their own (i.e. Barrister's fees, expert's fees and Court fees).

Disclosure

The exchange of relevant documents between each party in a case. Disclosure applies to all documents relevant to the case.

Disclosure List

A list which identifies the documents for disclosure in a chronological order. Each party in the litigation must provide a list and exchange them.

Disclosure Statement

A statement used to certify that a person giving Disclosure understands their legal obligations to disclose the relevant documents, confirm the extent of the search made for the documents and that the party has carried out the tasks to the best of their knowledge. The statement is served with a Disclosure List.

District Judge

A full time Judge who deals with the majority of cases in the County Courts of England and Wales.

Estoppel

A rule of evidence (or rule of law) which prevents a person from denying the truth about a statement he has made (or prevents a person from denying facts that he has alleged to exist). The denial must have been acted upon by the person who wishes to take advantage of the estoppel or his position must have been altered as a result. There are different types of estoppel (estoppel by conduct, estoppel by deed and estoppel by record).

Fast-Track

The Court process for dealing with cases in a relatively short period of time (for cases where Claimants are seeking less than £25,000 but more than £5,000).

Fiduciary

A person who owes another person an obligation of loyalty and good faith.

Fiduciary Duty

An obligation to act in the best interests of another party (i.e. trustees' duties to trust beneficiaries)

Grounds

The reasons or points which are relied upon for validating a claim or defence.

High Court

The Court in England and Wales where more complex or substantial civil cases are dealt with. It is located in London (but some High Court trials take place outside London). The High Court is split into two main divisions:

    1.   Queen's Bench Division

    2.   Chancery Division

The *Queen's Bench Division* deals with actions relating to contract and civil wrongs (except where cases are allocated to the Chancery Division). *The Chancery Division* deals with corporate, personal insolvency disputes, business, trade and industry disputes, copyrights and patents and probate and so on. A third division exists called '*Family Division*' which deals with family proceedings such as divorce, amongst other matters.

High Court Judge

A Judge in the High Court of Justice in London. They represent the third highest level of Judge in the Courts of England and Wales.

House of Lords (see also 'Supreme Court UK')

The highest civil appeal Court in the UK which sits in Westminster, London. It has now been replaced by the Supreme Court and has the same function.

Inadequate Professional Service (IPS)

A failure by a Solicitor to provide the Client with the requisite level of service which the Client could reasonably expected to have received in the circumstances of their matter. It is not 'misconduct', as such.

Indemnity

A contractual promise to make good the loss sustained by a person as a consequence of an act or omission of another.

Injunction

A Court order requiring a person to do (or refrain from) doing a specific act.

Interim Order

An order made by a Court during the course of litigation but is not the final order. Interim orders are designed to give temporary relief to the applicant.

Interim Payment

A sum of money ordered to be paid by a Court where an issue of liability has been found. An interim payment usually relates to costs orders. These types of payment are likely to be made the subject of a Court order where the extent of the financial liability to a winning party is substantial. The Court may decide that an advance payment should be made before the final amount of costs have been determined.

Judicial Review

A Court process where a Judge reviews the lawfulness of a decision or an action taken by a public body. They provide a means of challenging the way a decision has been made.

King's Counsel (K.C.)

See under 'Queen's Counsel'.

Law Centre

Law Centres are non profit legal practices which provide free legal advice and representation to disadvantaged people. Centres are usually High Street based and can be found in England, Wales and Northern Ireland. If a Law Centre is not able to take on your case, it may be able to refer you elsewhere. For help locating a Law Centre and more information go to *www.lawcentres.org.uk*. Alternatively, you could contact the Citizens Advice Bureau in your area for help in finding a centre.

Law Society

The professional association which represents Solicitors in England and Wales. The Society provides services and support to Solicitors. In England and Wales, the SRA (Solicitors Regulations Authority) regulates Solicitors and is independent of The Law Society, even though the two organisations are linked. Scotland and Northern Ireland have separate Law Societies. [**Scotland** - The Law Society of Scotland was established by the Legal Aid & Solicitors (Scotland) Act in 1949 and the main aims of the Society are set out in The Solicitors (Scotland) Act 1980. **Northern Ireland** - The Law Society of Northern Ireland was set up by Royal Charter in 1922 and incorporated under the 1976 Solicitors (Northern Ireland) Order].

Lawyer

A Solicitor or Barrister in the legal system. It is sometimes loosely used by individuals working in the legal profession to describe themselves when they are not actually Solicitors. A lay-person may not be aware of this and should check to see if the individual in question is a qualified Solicitor.

LawWorks

A charitable operation which helps find free legal assistance from volunteer Solicitors to those who cannot afford to pay. Assistance from the LawWorks organisation can be applied for through an Advice Agency (i.e. Citizen's Advice Bureau or Law Centre). Further details can be found at *www.lawworks.org.uk* or at **LawWorks (Solicitors' Pro Bono Group)**, The National Pro Bono Centre, 48 Chancery Lane, London WC2A 1JF. Telephone 0207 092 3940. PLEASE BEAR IN MIND THAT LAWWORKS IS A CHARITABLE ORGANISATION AND HAS LIMITED

RESOURCES. THE WORK WHICH IT CARRIES OUT IS INVALUABLE TO THE PEOPLE IT HELPS. LAWWORKS IS GRATEFUL FOR CHARITABLE DONATIONS.

Legal Aid

Financial aid provided by an organisation to serve the legal needs of people who cannot afford to employ/retain their own Counsel.

Legal Executive

A trained legal professional who may specialise in an area of law but who is not a qualified Solicitor. They work under the supervision of a Solicitor.

Legal Ombudsman

An independent organisation with official powers to resolve complaints about legal services in England and Wales. The organisation can help where an issue has not been resolved between an individual and their Solicitor. The organisation can be contacted on 0300 555 0333 (or +44 121 245 3050 if calling from overseas). Their address is: Legal Ombudsman, PO Box 6806, Wolverhampton WV1 9WJ (*enquiries@legalombudsman.org.uk*).

Lien

A security taken in property (relating to possession of it). For example, files taken by a Solicitor from a Client may be held under a 'lien' if a Client fails to pay their fees. The Solicitor is not entitled to dispose of or sell the property. They are simply entitled to maintain possession until such time the debt is paid.

Lord Chief Justice

The head of the judiciary of England and Wales.

Lord Justice

An ordinary Judge of the Court of Appeal of England and Wales.

Master of The Rolls

One of the Heads of Division of the Judiciary. He or she is also the leading Judge dealing with the civil work of the Court of Appeal. Historically, the Master of the Rolls was originally responsible for the safekeeping of charters, patents and records written on parchment rolls. The Master is still responsible for documents of national importance. The Master is regarded as the second in judicial importance to the Lord Chief Justice. He or she admits Solicitors to practice.

Mediation
See under 'Alternative Dispute Resolution'.

Multi-Track
The normal track in Court for cases falling outside the rules for allocation to either the 'Small Claims Track' or 'Fast-Track'. Typically, the 'Multi-Track' will be for cases involving claims exceeding £25,000 (and cases worth less than that sum where the trial is likely to exceed a day).

Notary (Notary Public)
A legal practitioner (usually a Solicitor) who certifies deeds and other legal documents.

Off the Record
A term used by Solicitors to describe a situation where they are no longer 'on record' as acting for a Client in a case (i.e. where they stop acting for you). Being on (or off) the record actually refers to your Solicitor being on the Court record as acting for you.

On the Record
A term used by Solicitors to describe a situation where they are 'on record' as acting for a Client on a case (i.e. they are acting for you). Being on (or off) the record actually refers to your Solicitor being on the Court record as acting for you.

Paralegal
A person, usually with some legal training but who has not gained a law degree or qualified as a Solicitor. They work under the supervision of a Solicitor. They are sometimes called Legal Assistants.

Particulars of Claim (POC)
The POC in English litigation is a statement of facts attached to the Claim Form which sets out the causes of action which a Claimant intends to press against the Defendant in litigation. The POC must contain a statement of the nature of the claim, remedies which the Claimant seeks from the Court, the sum of money claimed and interest and so on.

Pleadings
The written statement of facts and law filed by both parties in a law suit. They are now usually referred to as '**Statements of Case**'.

Points of Dispute

A set of points of issue or dispute prepared by a Costs Draftsman when legal costs are being assessed.

Pre-Action Disclosure

A means of providing the Claimant with the opportunity to obtain copies of documents from the intended Defendant to properly assess whether or not proceedings should be commenced. Usually, parties to civil litigations must wait for full Disclosure to inspect the documents but this is an alternative way.

Pre-Action Protocol Letter

A letter written by your Solicitor (usually in conjunction with Counsel) to a Defendant (or Defendant's Solicitor) which sets out the grounds for a pending legal action.

Queen's Bench Division

See under 'High Court'.

Queen's Counsel (Q.C.)

A Barrister that has been appointed Counsel to Her Majesty on the recommendation of the Lord Chancellor. The Barrister can also be known as 'King's Counsel' (K.C.), depending on the reign of the Monarch.

Recorders (Civil)

Individuals who sit as fee-paid Judges in County Courts. Some recorders may be authorised to stand in for civil Circuit Judges. In general, their role is similar to that of Circuit Judges but they do not usually hear appeals from District Judges. Cases a recorder might handle include housing disputes, commercial landlord and tenants, contract, tort or personal injury.

Refresher (s)

A term used to describe the fee paid to Counsel for attending a Court hearing. It is the fee paid each day when he or she appears in Court to argue your case. It is separate from a 'brief fee'.

Reply

The response by a party to a Defence.

Respondent

In English litigation, the Respondent is the legal person against whom an application or an appeal is made. The person filing an application notice is known as the 'Applicant'. A person bringing the appeal is the 'Appellant' and the person defending the appeal is the 'Respondent'.

Retainer

The contract between a Solicitor and a Client.

Senior Advocate

[Scottish Law] The equivalent to 'Queen's Counsel' (Q.C.) in Scottish law. They have a higher legal rank in Scotland than Advocates.

Sheriff

The exact meaning of the term varies between country to country and even region to region. Essentially, in England and Wales a 'Sheriff' is a law enforcement officer. In Scotland a 'Sheriff' is a Judge appointed on the recommendation of the Judicial Appointments Board for Scotland. They hear cases in Sheriff Courts. They are usually assigned to work in a specific Court although some do work anywhere in Scotland.

Sheriff Court

[Scottish Law] Courts providing a local service in Scotland with each Court serving a Sheriff Court District within a Sheriffdom. These Courts deal with civil actions and small claims procedures as well as adoption and bankruptcy.

Sheriffdom

[Scottish Law] One of the Sheriffdoms in Scotland. Each has a Sheriff Principal. Within each Sheriffdom there are Court Districts, each with a Court presided over by one or more Sheriffs. The Sheriffdoms are spread around the Scottish Districts.

Small Claims Court

A Court of limited jurisdiction which hears civil cases between private litigants with claims of small value.

Small Claims Track

The Court process for dealing with cases involving small sums of money (i.e. up to £10,000 – although this limit is due to be raised in the future, possibly up to £15,000).

Solicitor

A qualified professional person who offers legal services to Clients. They must be admitted by 'The Master of the Rolls' and hold a valid Practice

Certificate issued by The Law Society to be able to call themselves a Solicitor.

Solicitor Advocate

A Solicitor who has been granted the right to appear in the highest Courts. The term is usually used in Scottish law.

Solicitors Regulation Authority (SRA)

The SRA regulates Solicitors in England and Wales. The purpose of the organisation is to protect the public by ensuring that Solicitors meet high standards and by acting when risks are identified. The SRA is the independent regulatory body of The Law Society of England and Wales. The SRA carries out statutory functions in respect of a Solicitor's admission to practice, their conduct and the discipline of Solicitors. The SRA issues Practice Certificates to Solicitors (without which a Solicitor cannot practice) and it has the power to strike a Solicitor's name off the rolls or take disciplinary action. The Society is also responsible for setting the exams for people who intend to become Solicitors. The SRA actively deals with the regulatory and disciplinary matters. More information can be found at *www.sra.org.uk*.

Statements of Case

Please see under '**Pleadings**'

Summary Judgment

A process available to a Claimant or Defendant where there is no real prospect of a claim succeeding. The Court may give a Summary Judgment against a Claimant or Defendant on the whole claim (or on a particular issue) if it considers that the Claimant or Defendant has no real prospect of success on the claim or defence and there is no other compelling reason why the case should proceed to be dealt with at trial.

Supreme Court (UK)

The highest civil appeal Court in the UK which sits in London. The Court replaced the appeal function of the House of Lords in 2009 where the Law Lords previously sat in the Palace of Westminster.

Taxation

See under 'Assessment'.

Tort

The term used to describe a situation where a person or entity causes a civil wrong or injury. It comes from the Latin word 'tortus' which means 'wrong'.

Without Prejudice

A phrase used to enable parties in an action to negotiate a settlement without implying an admission of guilt or wrong doing. For example, letters and documents marked 'Without Prejudice' cannot be used as evidence in any Court action without the consent of both parties. Sometimes they can be used as evidence when costs are discussed in Court.

Witness Statement

A statement made by a witness (including Claimants and Defendants) which proves evidence to a Court in legal proceedings. It is a statement of facts made within the personal knowledge and belief of the person making the witness statement. It must follow a prescribed format and must be verified by a statement of truth.

Writ

A formal order directing a person to do (or not to do) a specified act.

p 43 = steps in the action from client's perspective

CPSIA information can be obtained at www.ICGtesting.com
Printed in the USA
BVOW06s0916060916

461263BV00008B/41/P